Preface

The greater part of the subject-matter of this volume was originally given as a lecture to the officers at the U. S. Infantry and Cavalry School. The kindly reception accorded to the lecture has encouraged me to revise and amplify it, and to publish it in its present form.

As to the narrative portion of the book, no other claim is made than that it is based upon the story of the campaign as given in the Prussian Official History of the Campaign of 1866, Hozier's *Seven Weeks' War*, Derrécagaix's *La Guerre Moderne*, and Adams' *Great Campaigns in Europe*. I have not deemed it necessary to cumber the pages with notes of reference, but will here express my indebtedness to the works mentioned, giving precedence to them in the order named. Other works have been consulted, which are enumerated in the bibliographical note at the end of the volume. I have also personally visited the scene of the operations described, and, especially in regard to the topography of the battlefield of Königgrätz, I am able to speak from my own observation.

My object has been:

1. To give a brief, but accurate, historical sketch of a great campaign, to which but little attention has been given in this country.

2. To make a comparison of some of the military features of the War of Secession with corresponding features of the European war which occurred one year later.

European critics have generally been loath to acknowledge the military excellence displayed during the War of Secession; and, even when giving full credit for the valour exhibited by our soldiers, have too often regarded our veteran armies as mere "armed mobs." Chesney, Adams, Trench and Maude have recognized the value of the lessons taught by the American armies, and Lord Wolseley has recently developed an appreciation of such American generalship and soldierly worth as he can see through Confederate spectacles. But European military writers generally, and those of the Continent especially, still fail to recognize in the developments of our war the germ, if not the prototype, of military features which are regarded as new in Europe. The remarks of Colonel Chesney still hold true:

> There is a disposition to regard the American generals, and the troops they led, as altogether inferior to regular soldiers. This prejudice was born out of the blunders and want of coherence exhibited by undisciplined volunteers at the outset—faults amply atoned for by the stubborn courage displayed by both sides throughout the rest of the struggle; while, if a man's claims to be regarded as a veteran are to be measured by the amount of actual fighting he has gone through, the most seasoned soldiers of Europe are but as conscripts compared with the survivors of that conflict. The conditions of war on a grand scale were illustrated to the full as much in the contest in America, as in those more recently waged on the Continent.

But it is not only among European critics that the military excellence displayed by our armies has been depreciated. There is a small class among the professional soldiers in our own country, who are wont to bestow all possible admiration upon the military operations in recent European wars, not because they were excellent, but because they were European; and to belittle the operations in our own war, not because they were not excellent, but because they were American. To this small class, whose humility in regard to our national achievements is rarely combined with individual modesty, this book is not addressed. It is to the true American soldier that this little volume is offered, with the hope that the views expressed may meet with his approval and be sanctioned by his judgment.

A. L. W.

Königgrätz: 1866

Königgrätz: 1866
The Epic Conflict of the Seven Week's War between Prussia & Austria

The Campaign of Königgrätz

Arthur L. Wagner

With a Short Illustrated Account of the
Battle of Königgrätz
by Charles Lowe

LEONAUR

Königgrätz: 1866
The Epic Conflict of the Seven Week's War between Prussia & Austria
The Campaign of Königgrätz
by Arthur L. Wagner
With a Short Illustrated Account of the Battle of Königgrätz
by Charles Lowe

FIRST EDITION

Leonaur is an imprint of Oakpast Ltd

Copyright in this form © 2016 Oakpast Ltd

ISBN: 978-1-78282-586-9 (hardcover)
ISBN: 978-1-78282-587-6 (softcover)

http://www.leonaur.com

Publisher's Notes

Contents

The Campaign of Königgrätz

THE MILITARY STRENGTH OF THE OPPOSING NATIONS

The German war of 1866, generally known as "the Seven Weeks' War," presents many features of interest to the student, the statesman and the soldier. It closed a strife of centuries between opposing nations and antagonistic political ideas. It resulted in the formation of the North German Confederation, and thus planted the seeds of a nation, which germinated four years later, during the bloody war with France. It banished Austria from all participation in the affairs of Germany, expelled her from Italy, and deflected her policy thenceforth towards the east and south. It demonstrated that preparation for war is a more potent factor than mere numbers in computing the strength of a nation; and it gave an illustration on a grand scale of the new conditions of war resulting from the use of the telegraph, the railroad and breech-loading firearms.

It is not the intention here to consider any but the military features of the great Germanic contest. Beginning the subject at the period when the quarrel between Austria and Prussia over the provinces that they had wrested from Denmark, passed from the tortuous paths of diplomacy to the direct road of war, we will consider the relative strength of the combatant nations.

As the advocate of the admission of Schleswig-Holstein as a sovereign state in the Germanic Confederation, Austria gained first the sympathy, and then the active alliance, of Bavaria, Hanover, Saxony, Hesse-Cassel, Würtemberg, Baden, Hesse-Darmstadt and Nassau. Prussia aimed at the incorporation of the duchies within her own territory; and, though loudly championing the cause of German unity, her course was so manifestly inspired by designs for her own aggrandizement, that she could count on the support of only a few petty duchies, whose aggregate military strength did not exceed 28,000

MAP

OF

GERMANY

PREVIOUS TO THE WAR OF 1866.

Scale of English Miles.

REFERENCE.

A *Anhalt* B *Brunswick* H *Hanover* H C *Hesse Cassel*
H D H° *Darmstadt* H H H° *Homburg* L *Lippe* OL *Oldenburg*
P *Prussia* R *Reuss* S *Schwarzburg* SA *Saxe Altenburg*
SC *and* SG *S.¹ Coburg & Gotha* SW *S.¹ Weimar* W *Waldeck*
Fortresses 1ˢᵗ *Class* ⊕ 2ⁿᵈ ⊙ 3ʳᵈ ⊗   *Forts* ◦
Railways ————

BOUNDARIES.

Prussia	——— ———
Other States	— — — —
Provinces	··········

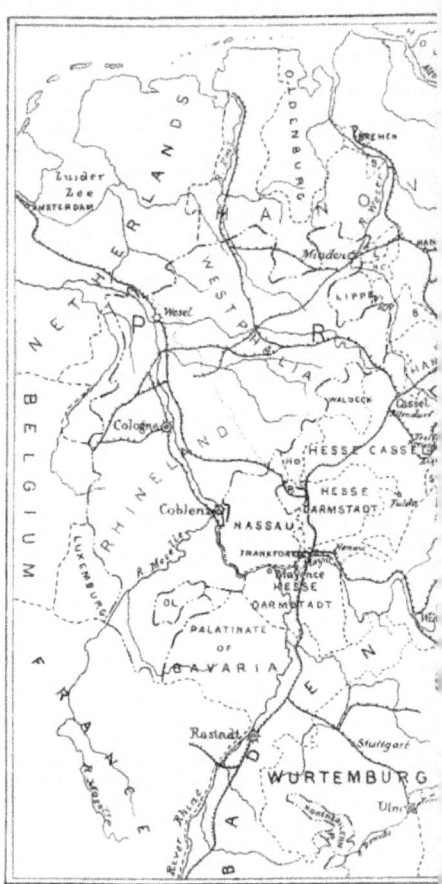

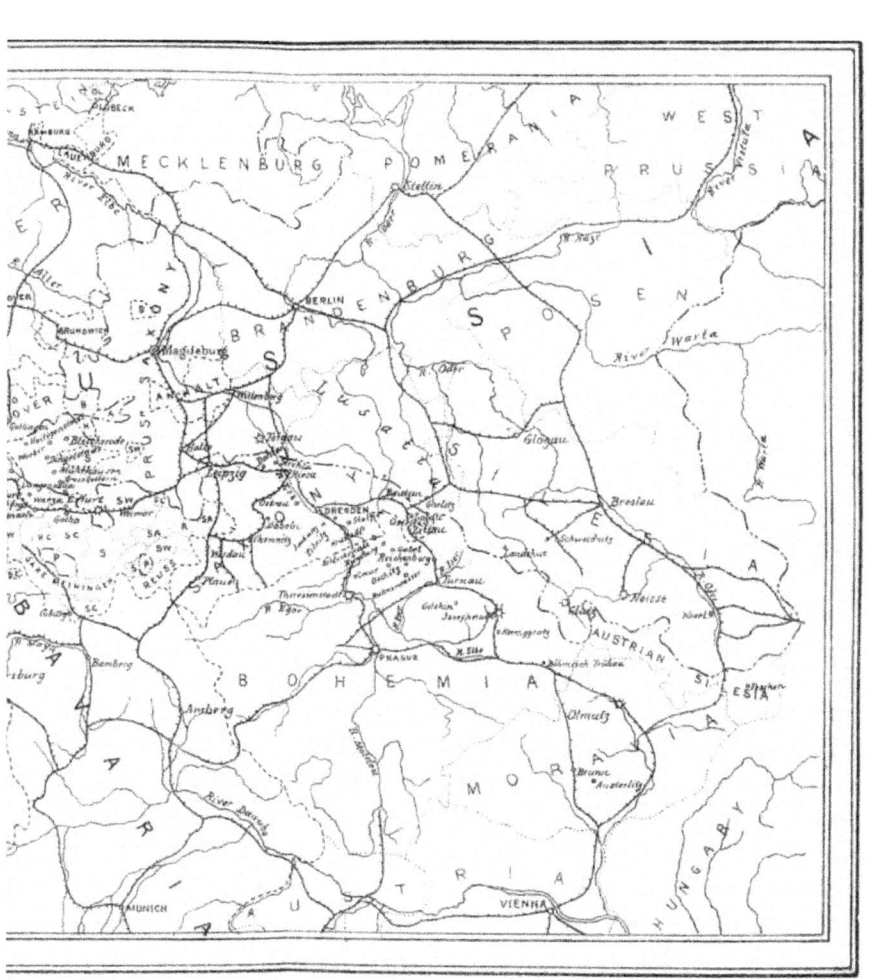

men. As an offset to Austria's formidable German allies, Prussia had concluded an offensive and defensive alliance with Italy, whose army, though new and inferior in organisation, armament and equipment, to that of her antagonist, might be relied upon to "contain" at least three Austrian Army corps in Venetia. The main struggle was certain to be between the two great Germanic nations.

At a first glance Prussia would seem to be almost hopelessly over-matched in her contest with Austria. The latter nation possessed an area more than twice as great as the former, and in contrast with the Prussian population of less than 20,000,000, it could show an aggregate of 35,000,000 people. But a more careful examination discloses the great superiority of the Prussian kingdom. The population of Prussia was almost exclusively German; that of Austria was a heterogeneous aggregation of Germans, Czechs, Magyars, Poles, Croats and Italians, bound together in a purely artificial nationality. The Austrian national debt amounted to nearly $1,550,000,000; the annual expenditures so far exceeded the revenue as to cause a yearly deficit of more than $16,000,000, and the nation was threatened with bankruptcy. On the other hand, the Prussian national debt was only $210,000,000, the revenue exceeded the expenditures, and the finances were in a healthy condition. But the great superiority of the northern kingdom over its opponent lay in the organisation, armament, equipment and *personnel* of its army.

The old adage, *"Experience is a severe, but good, schoolmaster,"* is true of nations as well as individuals. A crushing disaster, bringing with it humiliation, sorrow and disgrace, is often the birth of a stronger, better, life in the apparent victim of misfortune. The greatness of Prussia was not born in the brilliant victories of Rossbach, Leuthen and Zorndorf. It was in the bitter travail of Jena and the treaty of Tilsit that birth was given to the power of the kingdom. Forbidden by Napoleon to maintain an army of more than 42,000 men, the great Prussian war minister, Scharnhorst, determined to create an army while obeying the commands of the conqueror. There was no stipulation in the treaty as to the length of service of the soldiers; and after a few months of careful instruction and almost incessant drill, they were quietly discharged, and their places were taken by recruits, who were soon replaced in the same manner.

Thus the little army became, as it were, a lake of military training, into which flowed a continuous stream of recruits, and from which there came a steady current of efficient soldiers. When the army of

Napoleon returned from its disastrous campaign in Russia, there arose, as by magic, a formidable Prussian army, of which nearly 100,000 men were trained warriors.

The success of the Prussian arms in the final struggle with Napoleon was so manifestly due to the measures adopted by Scharnhorst, that his system was made the permanent basis of the national military policy. The "Reorganisation of 1859" nearly doubled the standing army, and made some important changes in the length of service required with the colours and in the *Landwehr,* but the essential features of the Prussian system are the same now as in the days of Leipsic and Waterloo.

Every Prussian twenty years of age is subject to military duty. The term of service is twelve years, of which three are with the colours, four with the reserve and five in the *Landwehr.* The number of soldiers in the active army is definitely fixed at a little more than one *per cent* of the population, and the number of recruits annually required is regulated by the number of men necessary to keep the regular force on its authorized peace footing. A list of the young men available for military service is annually made out, and the selection of recruits is made by lot. There are but few exceptions; such, for instance, as young men who are the sole support of indigent parents. Students who are preparing for the learned professions are permitted to serve as "one-year volunteers," on condition of passing certain examinations satisfactorily, and furnishing their own clothing and equipments. The name of a man convicted of crime is never placed on the list of available recruits; and however humble the position of a private soldier may be, his uniform is the honourable badge of an honest man.

Every young man may be called up for draft three years in succession. Those who are not drawn for service at the end of the third year are passed into the Ersatz reserve, in which are also men whose physical imperfections are not sufficient to exempt them entirely, where they are free from service in time of peace, but from which they may be called in time of war to replace drafts from the reserve. In time of peace the military demands upon the soldiers of the reserve or Landwehr are very light. A soldier participates in at least two field manoeuvres, aggregating about sixteen weeks, during his four years of service in the reserve. He is also required to attend muster once every spring and autumn. During his five years in the *Landwehr* he is generally called out twice for drill, the drill period not exceeding fourteen days.

The active army is the regular army, or permanent establishment. When the decree for the mobilisation of the army is promulgated, this force is at once put upon its war footing by drafts from the reserve. The depots are immediately formed, and one-half of the troops stationed therein are drawn from the reserve; the other half being recruits from the Ersatz reserve. As these two classes become exhausted, the depot battalions are filled from the *Landwehr*, the youngest classes being taken first; or, if needs be, the entire *Landwehr* is called out in battalions, regiments, brigades, divisions, or even army corps, and sent into the field. After exhausting the *Landwehr*, there still remains the *Landsturm*, which embraces all able-bodied men between the ages of seventeen and forty-nine years who do not belong to the active army, the reserve, or the *Landwehr*. Though the calling out of the *Landsturm* would imply the exhaustion of the organised forces of the nation, it would be more than a mere levy *en masse*, as it would bring back into the army many soldiers whose twelve years of service would not have been completely forgotten in the midst of civil vocations.

The machinery for the rapid mobilisation of the army is kept in perfect order. Each army corps, except the Guards, is assigned to a particular province. The province is divided into divisional districts, which are again subdivided so that each brigade, regiment and battalion has its own district, from which it draws its recruits both in peace and war. A register is kept of every man available for military duty, and in time of peace every officer knows just what part he is to perform the minute mobilisation is decreed, and each soldier knows where he is to report for duty. The secret of the efficiency of the German military system lies in the division of responsibility, and the thorough decentralization, by which every man, from the monarch to the private soldier, has his own especial part to perform.

In 1866 the active army, on a war footing, comprised nine army corps, and aggregated 335,000 men. Each corps consisted of twenty-four battalions of infantry, sixteen batteries of artillery, twenty-four squadrons of cavalry, one battalion of rifles, one battalion of engineers, an engineer train, and a military train conveying ammunition and subsistence, quartermaster's and hospital supplies. Each infantry battalion numbered 1,000 men. Three battalions formed a regiment, two regiments a brigade, and two brigades a division. Each battery contained six guns. Four batteries were assigned to each infantry division, two batteries of horse artillery were attached to the cavalry division, and four batteries of field and two of horse artillery constituted the reserve artillery of each corps. Each squadron of cavalry numbered about 140 sabres. Four squadrons composed a regiment, two regiments a brigade, two brigades a division. A regiment of cavalry was attached to each infantry division. Each corps numbered about 31,000 combatants, except the Guards, which numbered 36,000—having four additional battalions and eight additional squadrons. During the campaign under consideration, the cavalry of an army corps consisted of only one regiment to each division of infantry; the cavalry division being taken from each corps, and merged into the corps of reserve cavalry.

The depot troops consisted of a battalion for each regiment of infantry, a squadron for each regiment of cavalry, an *abtheilung* (3 or 4 batteries) for the artillery of each corps, and a company for each rifle battalion, engineer battalion and train battalion. The army in the field was constantly kept up to a full war strength by men drawn from the depots. The fortresses were garrisoned by *Landwehr*; and on troops of the same class devolved the duty of pushing forward to occupy invaded territory, and to relieve the active army from the necessity of leaving detachments to guard its communications.

This is a brief outline of the organisation that enabled a nation of less than 20,000,000 people eventually to bring 600,000 soldiers upon the theatre of war, and to place a quarter of a million of them upon the decisive field of Königgrätz.

The Austrian regular army, when placed upon its war footing, numbered about 384,000 men; and by calling out all of the reserve, this force could be raised to a formidable total of 700,000. But in organisation and system of recruitment the Austrian Army was inferior to its antagonist, notwithstanding its war experience in 1849 and in the struggle with France and Italy ten years later. The superb system by which Prussia was enabled to send forth a steady stream of trained soldiers to replace the losses of battle was wanting in Austria; and the machinery of military administration seemed deranged by the effort required to place the first gigantic armies in the field. The difference between the two military systems is shown in a striking manner by the fact that the mobilisation of the Prussian Army of 490,000 men, decreed early in May, was completed in fourteen days, and by the 5th of June 325,000 were massed on the hostile frontiers; while the mobilisation of the Austrian Army, begun ten weeks earlier than that of Prussia, was far from complete on that date.

Nor was the superiority of the Prussian to the Austrian Army, as a collective body, greater than the individual superiority of the Prussian soldier to his antagonist. As a result of the admirable Prussian school system, every Prussian soldier was an educated man. Baron Stoffel, the

French military *attaché* at Berlin from 1866 to 1870, says:

> 'When,' said the Prussian officers, 'our men came in contact with the Austrian prisoners, and on speaking to them found that they hardly knew their right hand from their left, there was not one who did not look upon himself as a god in comparison with such ignorant beings, and this conviction increased our strength tenfold.'

The Prussian Army was the first that ever took the field armed entirely with breech-loading firearms. In the War of Secession, a portion of the Federal troops were, towards the end of the struggle, armed with breech-loading rifles; but now the entire Prussian Army marched forth with breech-loaders, to battle against an army which still retained the muzzle-loading rifle. Great as was the superiority of the needle gun over the Austrian musket, it would seem but a sorry weapon at the present day. The breech mechanism was clumsy, the cartridge case was made of paper, the accuracy of the rifle did not extend beyond 300 yards, and its extreme range was scarcely more than twice that distance.

Yet this rifle was the best infantry weapon of the time, and it contributed greatly to the success of the Prussians. The Prussian artillery was armed mainly with steel breech-loading rifled guns. These guns were classed as 6-pounders and 4-pounders, though the larger piece fired a shell weighing 15 lbs., and the smaller one used a similar projectile weighing 9 lbs.

★★★★★★

> These guns were classed, not according to the weight of the projectile, but according to the diameter of the bore. Thus the gun firing a 15-lb. shell was rated as a 6-pdr., because the diameter of its bore was the same as that of a 6-pdr. smooth-bore gun.

★★★★★★

Shell fire seems to have been exclusively used, and the shells to have been uniformly provided with percussion fuses.

In the Austrian Army the artillery was provided with bronze muzzle-loading rifled guns, classified as 8-pdrs. and 4-pdrs. The infantry was armed with the muzzle-loading Lorenz rifle.

The German allies of Austria could place about 150,000 men in the field; Italy, about 200,000.

The geographical situation was unfavourable to Prussia. The map of Germany, as it existed before the Austro-Prussian war, shows Rhineland and Westphalia completely separated from the other provinces of Prussia by the hostile territory of Hanover and Hesse-Cassel, which, extending from the north, joined the South German States which were in arms against the northern kingdom. The Austrian province of Bohemia, with the adjacent kingdom of Saxony, formed a salient, pushing forward, as it were, into the Prussian dominions, and furnishing a base from which either Silesia or Lusatia might be invaded. In the language of the Prussian Staff History of the Campaign of 1866:

> In one direction stood the Saxon Army as a powerful advanced guard only six or seven marches distant from the Prussian capital, which is protected from the south by no considerable vantage ground; in the other Breslau could the more easily be reached in five marches, because, trusting to a former federal compact with Austria, Schweidnitz had been given up as a fortress.

The forces of Hanover and Hesse-Cassel, numbering 25,000 men, could operate against the communications of the Prussian Armies, or withdraw to the south and unite with the Austrians or Bavarians. The South German Armies might form a junction in Saxony or Bohemia with the Austro-Saxon Army.

The Plans of Von Moltke and Von Benedek, and the Dispositions of the Opposing Armies.

The Prussian Army was commanded by the king. His chief-of-staff was Baron Hellmuth Von Moltke, a soldier of reputation in Prussia, but as yet almost unknown beyond the boundaries of his own country.

The object of Von Moltke was to protect the Prussian rear by defeating the Hanoverian and Hessian troops; to prevent a junction of these troops with their South German allies; to "contain" the latter with as small a force as possible, and to hurl the crushing weight of the Prussian forces upon the Austro-Saxon Army.

On the 14th of June the Prussian Armies were stationed as follows:

The "Army of the Elbe," consisting of three divisions, two cavalry brigades and 144 guns, in cantonments round Torgau, under command of General Herwarth Von Bittenfeld;

The "First Army," consisting of three army corps, a cavalry corps of six brigades, and 300 guns, near Görlitz, under command of Prince

Frederick Charles;

The "Second Army," consisting of four army corps, a cavalry division of three brigades, and 336 guns, in the vicinity of Neisse, under command of the Crown prince.

Besides the three main armies, there were other forces stationed as follows:

One division at Altona, in Holstein, under Von Manteuffel;

One division at Minden, under Vogel Von Falckenstein;

One division (made up principally of the Prussian garrisons withdrawn from the Federal fortresses of Mayence, Rastadt and Frankfort) at Wetzlar, under Von Beyer.

The Austrian "Army of the North" was posted as follows:

Ist Corps, at Prague, Teplitz, Theresienstadt and Josephstadt;

IInd Corps, near Bömisch Trübau;

IVth Corps, near Teschen;

VIth Corps, at Olmütz;

IIId Corps, at Brünn;

Xth Corps at Brünn;

VIIIth Corps, in the neighbourhood of Austerlitz.

To these corps were attached five divisions of cavalry and more than 750 guns.

This army was under command of Field Marshal Von Benedek, an officer of great experience and high reputation.

The Saxon Army, 25,000 strong, with fifty-eight guns, was at Dresden, under command of the Crown prince of Saxony.

The Bavarian Army was concentrating on the line of the Main between Amberg and Würzburg. It numbered 52,000 men, and was under command of Prince Charles of Bavaria.

The VIIIth Federal Corps was forming at Frankfort. It consisted of the contingents of Würtemberg, Baden, Hesse-Darmstadt and Nassau, and an Austrian division drawn from the Federal fortresses. It numbered about 42,000 men, and was under the command of Prince Alexander of Hesse.

The Vth, VIIth and IXth Austrian corps, under the Archduke Albrecht, were in Venetia, opposed to an Italian army of four corps.

Von Benedek expected to assume the offensive and invade Prussia.

He had announced this intention before the beginning of hostilities, even going so far as to prescribe rules for the behaviour of his soldiers while in the enemy's country. It is hard to understand (in the light of subsequent events) the slight esteem in which the Austrians held their opponents before the commencement of hostilities. In a general order issued to his army on June 17, 1866, the Austrian commander says:

> We are now faced by inimical forces, composed partly of troops of the line and partly of *Landwehr*. The first comprises young men not accustomed to privations and fatigue, and who have never yet made an important campaign; the latter is composed of doubtful and dissatisfied elements, which, rather than fight against us, would prefer the downfall of their government. In consequence of a long course of years of peace, the enemy does not possess a single general who has had an opportunity of learning his duties on the field of battle.

Von Benedek's unfavourable opinion of his adversaries was probably shared by many other prominent European soldiers; for the excellence of the military system of Prussia was, as yet, not appreciated by other nations. Absurd as Von Benedek's order now appears, it seems to have excited no unfavourable comment at the time of its appearance; and, in fact, the expectation of Austrian success was quite general in Europe.

On the 15th of June the Austrian outposts were notified of the intention of the Prussians to begin hostilities, and war was formally declared against Hanover, Hesse-Cassel and Saxony. Within twenty-four hours after the declaration of war, the invasion of each of these minor states was begun.

Operations Against the Hessians and Hanoverians.
(See earlier Map of Germany)

Von Falckenstein from Minden, and Von Manteuffel from Altona, moved upon Hanover, and Von Beyer invaded Hesse-Cassel from Wetzlar. On the night of the 15th the Hanoverian army, accompanied by the blind monarch, King George, retreated, chiefly by rail, to Göttingen; the retreat being conducted in such haste that even the reserve ammunition and hospital supplies were left behind. On the 17th Von Falckenstein entered the Hanoverian capital; on the 19th Von Manteuffel marched into the city; and by the 22nd all Hanover, except Göttingen, was in the possession of the Prussians.

Von Beyer pushed into Hesse-Cassel, the Hessian Army retiring before him, by way of Fulda, upon Hanau, where it formed a junction with the Federal forces. On the 19th the Prussians entered Cassel, and an army was thus placed across the path of the retreating Hanoverians.

The Hanoverian Army, which had been compelled to wait several days at Göttingen to complete its organisation, resumed its march on the 21st, intending to cross a portion of the Prussian territory *via* Heiligenstadt and Langensalza, and thence through Eisenach or Gotha, to form a junction with the Bavarians in the neighbourhood of Fulda. Von Falckenstein pursued from Hanover, detachments were sent from Magdeburg and Erfurt to Bleicherode and Eisenach, and Von Beyer occupied the line of the Werra between Allendorf and Eisenach. Though the route through Eisenach was thus blocked, energetic measures on the part of the allies might easily have extricated the Hanoverian Army from the constricting grasp of the Prussians.

Gotha was occupied by a weak force of six battalions, two squadrons and three batteries, while the retreating army numbered 20,500 men. Had the Bavarian Army been well prepared and ably led, a junction might have been formed with the Hanoverians, and the Prussian force at Gotha captured. But the Bavarian commander was inefficient, and the over-estimate placed by King George upon the number of his enemies at Gotha was strengthened by the receipt, from the commander of the petty force, of an audacious summons to surrender. Negotiations were entered upon by the Prussian and Hanoverian representatives; but the armistice (begun on the 24th and continued until the 26th) produced no other result than the reinforcement of the force at Gotha; General Von Flies, with five battalions, being detached from Von Falckenstein's army, and sent by rail, *via* Magdeburg and Halle, to Gotha.

At Treffurt, Kreutzberg, Eisenach and Gotha, points on a semi-circle in front of the Hanoverians, and within a day's march of them, were nearly 30,000 Prussians.

On the 27th General Von Flies, advancing through Warza upon Langensalza, with about 9,000 men, struck the army of King George, which was well posted on the left bank of the Unstrut River. A battle followed, in which the Hanoverians defeated Von Flies, and drove his army several miles towards Warza.

But the Hanoverian victory was a barren one. Von Flies was reinforced at Warza by a strong detachment from Von Goeben's division at Eisenach. Von Goeben and Von Beyer advanced from Eisenach upon

Langensalza, and Von Manteuffel, moving *via* Heiligenstadt, Worbis, Dingelstadt, Mühlhausen and Gross Gottern, closed upon the Hanoverians from the north. The army of King George was now surrounded by 40,000 Prussians, united under the command of Von Falckenstein. Further resistance was hopeless, and on the 29th of June the Hanoverians surrendered. The men were dismissed to their homes, the officers were paroled, and King George was banished from his kingdom.

The Invasion of Saxony, and Its Results.

In the meantime, the main armies had not been idle. The invasion of Saxony was begun on the 16th of June by the Army of the Elbe and the First Army. On the night of the 15th of June the Saxon army began its retreat to Bohemia, detachments of pioneers tearing up the railroad track between Rieza and Dresden, and between the latter city and Bautzen. The work of destruction, except the burning of the bridge at Rieza, was hurriedly and imperfectly done, and did not appreciably delay the Prussian advance. The Army of the Elbe advanced from Torgau, *via* Wurzen, Dahlen and Strehla; a division to each road, and a detachment from the right division moving *via* Ostrau and Dobeln to cover the right flank.

The First Army advanced from the neighbourhood of Görlitz, through Löbau and Bautzen, a strong detachment being sent out on the Zittau road, beyond Ostritz, to observe the passes of Reichenberg and Gabel, for the army was making a flank march, and the Austrians might attack through these passes. A cavalry detachment was pushed out through Bischofswerda to feel the left of the Army of the Elbe.

On the 18th of June the Army of the Elbe occupied Dresden, and pushed its outposts beyond the city as far as Lockwitz and Pillnitz. On the following day the junction of the two armies was perfected. The 1st Reserve Division was sent from Berlin to reinforce Herwarth Von Bittenfeld, and the combined forces of the Army of the Elbe and the First Army were placed under the command of Prince Frederick Charles. To guard against a possible invasion of Saxony by the Bavarians, measures were at once taken to fortify Dresden, which was occupied by the 2nd Reserve Division from Berlin; Leipsic and Chemnitz were occupied by Landwehr; and the Leipsic-Plauen railway beyond Werdau was destroyed.

On the 17th of June the Emperor of Austria issued a manifesto, in which he formally announced to his subjects the state of war existing between Austria and Prussia. Italy declared war against Austria three days later.

We can now see the immense results following from the thorough military preparation of Prussia. Launching, as it were, a thunderbolt of military force upon her enemies at the first moment of war, less than two weeks sufficed for the complete conquest of Hanover, Hesse-Cassel and Saxony. Indeed, four days had sufficed for the seizure of the last two. The King of Hanover had been dethroned; the Elector of Hesse-Cassel was a prisoner, and the King of Saxony was a fugitive with his army in Bohemia. The military results were even greater than the political consequences. The severed portions of the Prussian kingdom were united. The Hanoverian Army had been eliminated from the military problem, and there was no longer any menace to Prussia from the rear. Von Falckenstein was now free to turn his undivided attention to the Bavarians and the Federal Corps, and the occupation of Saxony prevented all possibility of a junction of the Bavarian and Saxon Armies. But the strategical advantages gained in regard to operations in Bohemia were the grandest result of the occupation of Saxony.

We have seen that on the 14th of June the Army of the Elbe was around Torgau, the First Army near Görlitz; and the Second Army in the vicinity of Neisse; being thus separated from each other by from 100 to 125 miles. The Second Army covered Breslau, the Army of the Elbe covered Berlin, and the First Army was in a position to support either of the others. Geographical circumstances thus compelled the separation of the Prussian armies, and only two of them were available for the invasion of Bohemia. The occupation of Saxony changed matters for the better. The distance between the Army of the Elbe and the First Army was reduced to the extent of actual junction, and these combined armies were only about 120 miles from Landshut, where the right of the Second Army now rested, and with which there was communication by means of the hill road of Schreiberschau. The entire force was now available for the invasion of Bohemia; the northern passes of the Bohemian frontier were secured; and if compelled to act upon the defensive, Frederick Charles could find in the mountains of Southern Saxony many advantageous positions for defensive battle.

The Prussian plan of operations required an advance of Frederick Charles' armies from Saxony into Bohemia, and an invasion of that province by the Second Army, advancing from Silesia; both armies to unite at Gitschin, or in its vicinity. It is clear that in thus advancing from divergent bases, the Prussians gave to their adversary the advantage of operating by interior lines; generally, a serious military error, as the general operating by interior lines, holding one of the opponent's armies by a containing force, and falling with superior numbers upon the other, may defeat both in succession. Von Moltke's plan was, however, sound and proper, for the following reasons:

1. The geographical configuration of the Prussian frontier compelled the separation of the Prussian armies, in order that Lusatia and Silesia might both be protected from Austrian invasion; and the only possible concentration that would not yield to the enemy the advantage of the initiative, and permit him to invade Prussia, was a concentration to the front, in the hostile territory.

2. The entire army "could not have advanced in effective order by one set of mountain roads, but would have extended in columns so lengthened that it would have been impossible to form to a front commensurate with its numbers."

3. The re-entering base of the Prussians would enable each of their armies to cover its communications with its base, while one of these armies would surely menace the communications of the Austrians, if Von Benedek should advance against either.

4. The certainty that the Prussian Armies could act with celerity, and the probability that the Austrian Army was not yet fully prepared for prompt offensive manoeuvres, justified the hope that the concentration might be effected at a point some distance in front of the enemy's line. The distance from Görlitz and Neisse to Gitschin was less than the distance from Olmütz, Brünn and Bömisch Trübau to the same point, and there was an excellent prospect of being able to concentrate before Von Benedek could get his army well in hand to strike the Prussian separately.

5. By keeping up telegraphic communication between the two separated armies, their co-operation and simultaneous action could be assured.

6. If the Prussians could reach the Iser and the Elbe without serious check, the contracted theatre of operations would render Von Benedek's interior position one of danger, rather than one of advantage. Von Moltke himself, in commenting upon his strategical combination, says:

> If it is advantageous for a general to place his army on an interior line of operation, it is necessary, in order that he may profit by it, to have sufficient space to enable him to move against

one of his adversaries at a distance of several days' march, and to have time enough then to return against the other. If this space is very contracted, he will run the risk of having both adversaries on his hands at once. When an army, on the field of battle, is attacked in front and on the flank, it avails nothing that it is on an interior line of operations. That which was a strategical advantage becomes a tactical disadvantage. If the Prussians were allowed to advance to the Iser and to the Elbe, if the several defiles which it was necessary to pass fell into their power, it is evident that it would be extremely perilous to advance between their two armies. In attacking one, the risk would be incurred of being attacked in rear by the other.

The combination, on the field of battle, of the two armies operating from divergent bases, would admit of just such a front and flank attack as would convert Von Benedek's strategical advantage into a serious tactical disadvantage. It would be a repetition of Waterloo.

7. A failure to unite before encountering the main force of the enemy, though unfortunate, would not necessarily have been disastrous. According to Jomini, the advantages of an interior position diminish as the armies operating increase in size; for the following reasons:

(a). Considering the difficulty of finding ground and time necessary to bring a very large force into action on the day of the battle, an army of 130,000 or 140,000 men may easily resist a much larger force.

(b). If driven from the field, there will be at least 100,000 men to protect and insure an orderly retreat and effect a junction with one of the other armies.

(c). The central army . . . . requires such a quantity of provisions, munitions, horses and *materiel* of every kind, that it will possess less mobility and facility in shifting its efforts from one part of the zone to another; to say nothing of the impossibility of obtaining provisions from a region too restricted to support such numbers.

(d). The bodies of observation detached from the central mass to hold in check two armies of 135,000 men each must be very strong (from 80,000 to 90,000 each); and, being of such magnitude, if they are drawn into a serious engagement, they will probably suffer reverses, the effect of which might outweigh the advantages gained by the principal army.

Finally, the increased defensive power given to infantry by the introduction of breech-loading rifles might be counted upon to increase greatly the probability of either of the Prussian armies being able to fight successfully a *purely defensive* battle against the entire army of Von Benedek, armed, as it was, with muzzle-loaders.

In view of these reasons, Von Moltke's strategy was not only justifiable, but perfect. The Prussian objective was the Austrian Army, wherever it might be.

Before the commencement of hostilities Von Benedek had, as we have seen, announced his intention of invading Prussia. Two routes offered themselves to his choice: one by way of Görlitz and Bautzen to Berlin; the other by way of the valley of the Oder into Silesia. The latter route was obstructed by the fortresses of Glatz, Neisse and Kosel; the former would have led to the unobstructed occupation of Saxony, and would have enabled the Bavarian army to concentrate, *via* the passes of the Saale and Wittenberg, with the Austrians and Saxons. But, at a time when minutes were worth millions, Von Benedek was slow; and the preparation and energy of the Prussians enabled them to take the initiative and throw the Austrians upon the defensive in Bohemia. Von Benedek then decided to concentrate his army in the vicinity of Josephstadt and Königinhof; to hold the strong defiles of the Iser or the Elbe with comparatively weak detachments, and throw his main army upon the crown prince or Frederick Charles, as circumstances might decide.

Von Benedek's concentration began on the 18th of June; and on the 25th his army stood as follows:

The Ist Corps, with one brigade of the IIIrd Corps and a cavalry division, on the left bank of the Iser, from Turnau, through Müchengrätz to Jung Buntzlau, where the retreating Saxons formed on the left.

The Xth Corps, with one cavalry division, at Jaromir.

The IVth Corps at Opocno.

The VIth Corps at Solnitz.

The IIIrd Corps on the left of the VIth, at Tynist.

The VIIIth Corps at Wamberg.

The IId Corps at Geyersberg.

Four cavalry divisions were at Gabel, Leitomischel, Abtsdorf and Policzka, respectively.

The force on the Iser, under Count Clam-Gallas, was thus opposed to the entire army of Frederick Charles; while Von Benedek confronted the crown prince with six corps. The Austrian line extended beyond Gitschin, the point at which the Prussian armies were to concentrate.

THE INVASION OF BOHEMIA.

It was now certain that Bohemia was to be the theatre of war. This province of the Austrian Empire may be described as a huge basin, whose rim is composed of mountains. It is separated from Silesia by the Riesengebirge (Giant Mountains), from Saxony by the Erzgebirge (Iron Mountains), from Moravia by the Moravian Hills, and from Bavaria by the Fichtelgebirge and the Böhmerwald; the Moravian Hills and the Böhmerwald separating it from the valley of the Danube. This great basin is drained by the Elbe River, which, rising in the Riesengebirge, makes a huge loop, flowing first south, then west, and finally north, and receives the waters of the Iser, Adler, Moldau and Eger Rivers before it issues forth from the Bohemian frontier into Saxony. This theatre is well suited to defensive operations, as the mountain frontiers are penetrated by few passes, and the forests and rivers constitute additional obstacles. On the Silesian frontier the only issues by which an invader can enter Bohemia are the passes of Trautenau, Eypel, Kosteletz, Nachod and Neustadt. These passes could all be easily defended, while on the Saxon frontier the passes of Reichenberg, Gabel and Königstein-Tetschen could be used by retarding forces, which could afterwards find a strong defensive line on the Iser.

Two railway lines lay in the theatre of war, and were of great importance to the contending armies. One line ran from Vienna, *via* Kosel, Breslau and Görlitz, to Dresden. The other connected the Austrian capital with Prague, *via* Olmütz (or Brünn) and Bömisch Trübau. The two lines were joined by a railway from Dresden to Prague, and by one which, running from Löbau to Turnau, branched from the latter point to Prague and Pardubitz. These railways connected with others leading to all the important cities of Prussia. The two Prussian armies could cover their railway communications while advancing; but the Prague-Olmütz line, which was of vital importance to the Austrian army, ran parallel to, and dangerously near, the Silesian frontier, and was not covered by the Austrian front during the operations in Bohemia.

The Prussian advance began on the 20th of June. The Army of the Elbe marched from the vicinity of Dresden, *via* Stolpen, Neustadt, Schluckenau and Rumburg, to Gabel. As the greater part of this march had to be made by one road, it required six days, though the distance was only 65 miles. The First Army had concentrated at Zittau, Herrnhut, Hirschfelde, Seidenberg and Marklissa. From these points it began its march on the 22nd of June, each division marching by a separate road; and on the 25th it was closely concentrated around Reichenberg. The entire Prussian front was now reduced to about 100 miles, and Herwarth Von Bittenfeld was only twelve miles from Frederick Charles.

It would have been dangerous in the extreme for the crown prince to begin his march while Von Benedek held six corps in hand to hurl upon him. The passage of the Second Army through the defiles depended on surprise; and in the face of a superior and concentrated army, it would have been a desperate undertaking. It was necessary, therefore, to distract the plans of the enemy by false manoeuvres, and to wait for Frederick Charles to menace the Austrian left, on the Iser, before beginning the forward movement with the Second Army. With these objects in view, the VIth Corps was ordered to push forward towards Olmütz, and Frederick Charles received the following instructions from Von Moltke:

> Since the difficult task of debouching from the mountains falls upon the Second, weaker, Army, so, as soon as the junction with Herwarth's corps is effected, the First Army must, by its rapid advance, shorten the crisis.

The VIth Corps moved from Neisse into the Austrian dominions as far as Freiwaldau, where its advanced-guard had a successful skirmish with a party of Austrian cavalry. This corps was supposed by the Austrians to be the advanced-guard of the crown prince's army marching upon Olmütz; and the demonstration had the effect of holding a large force of Austrians between Hohenmauth and Bömisch Trübau, where it could not be used to oppose the real advance of the Second Army.

★★★★★★

It may be of assistance to the reader, in the following pages, to note that the divisions in the Prussian Army are numbered consecutively throughout the several army corps. Thus, the Ist Corps consists of the 1st and 2nd Divisions; the IId Corps, of the 3rd and 4th Divisions; the VIth Corps, of the 11th and 12th Divisions, and so on.

★★★★★★

Herrnhut

Ostrit

Hirschfeld

Zittau

Reibersdo

Köhlige
Grottau Wanwa

Gabel

Pankraz

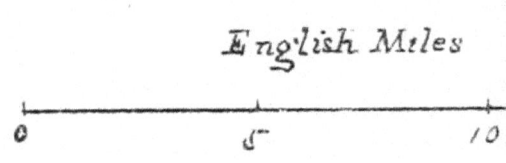

English Miles

0   5   10

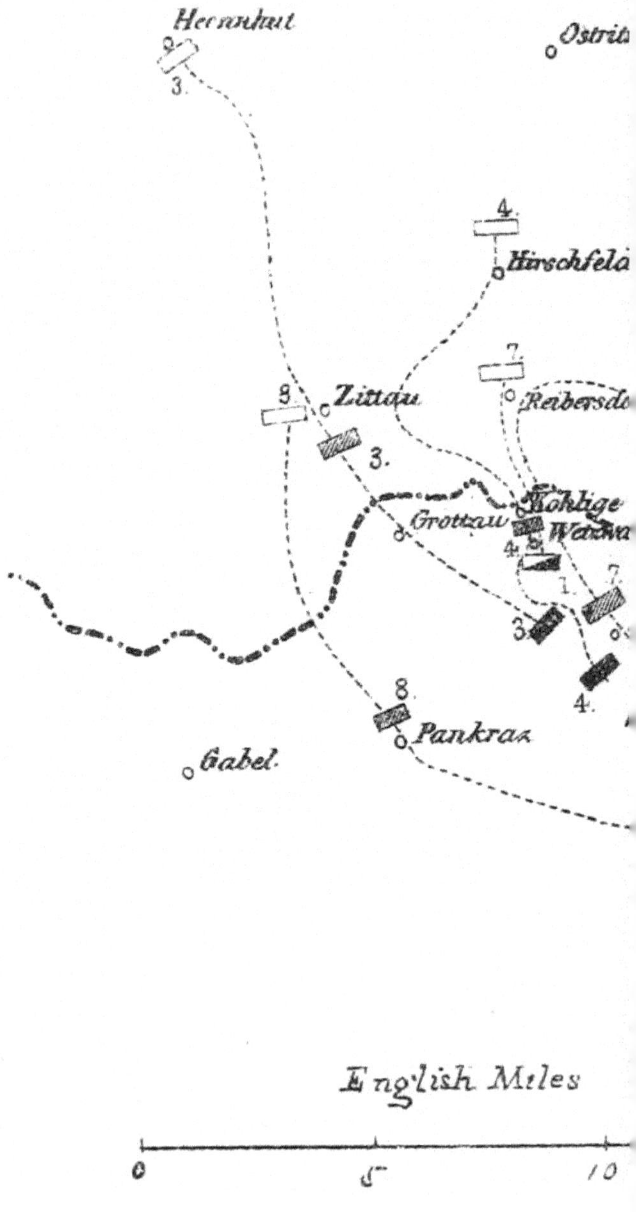

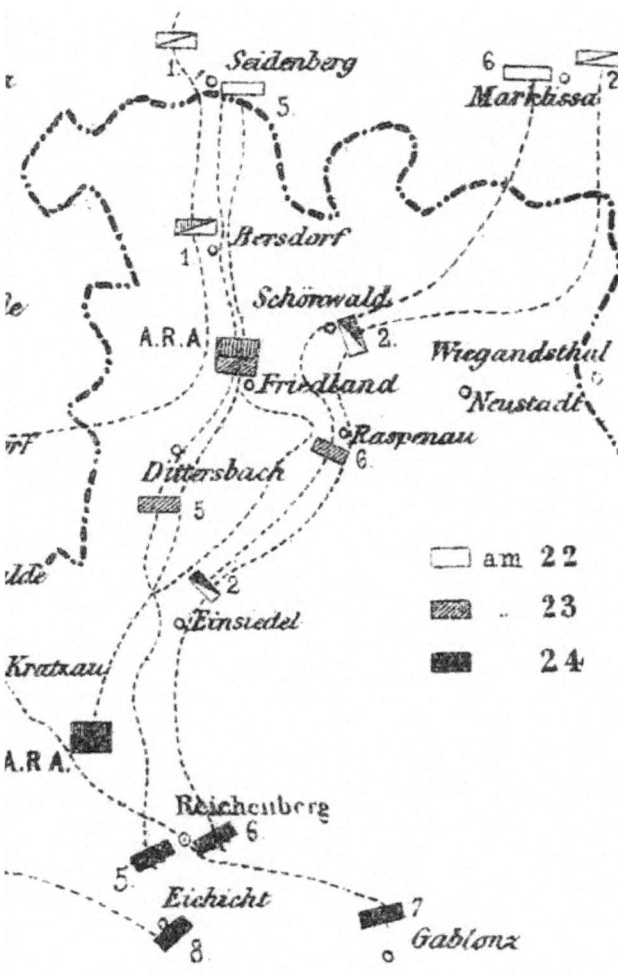

Seidenberg

Marklissa

6

2

1

5

Bersdorf

1

Schönwald

A.R.A.

2

Wiegandsthal

Fridland

Neustadt

Raspnau

6

Dittersbach

5

2

Einsiedel

Kratzau

A.R.A.

Reichenberg

6

5

Eichicht

7

Gablonz

8

	am 22
	" 23
	24

15

The crown prince's army was to move as follows:

The Ist Corps *via* Liebau and Trautenau, to Arnau;

The Guards, *via* Neurode, Braunau, Eypel, to Königinhof;

The Vth Corps, *via* Glatz, Reinerz, Nachod, to Gradlitz;

The cavalry, from Waldenburg, *via* Trautenau, to Königinhof.

The VIth Corps, having made the diversion to Freiwaldau, was withdrawn to Glatz and Patschkau, from which points it was to follow the Vth. A corps of observation, consisting of two regiments of infantry, one of cavalry, and a light battery, was detached at Ratibor to make demonstrations against Austrian Silesia. In case this detachment should encounter a large force of the enemy, it was to fall back upon the fortress of Kosel. During the campaign an unimportant war of detachments was carried on in this region, generally to the advantage of the Prussians.

JUNE 26TH.

On the 26th of June the Army of the Elbe marched upon Niemes and Oschitz. The advanced-guard encountered an Austrian outpost near Hühnerwasser, and drove it back after a sharp skirmish. The main body of the Army of the Elbe bivouacked at Hühnerwasser, with outposts towards Weisswasser, Münchengrätz and Gablonz. In the evening there was another brisk outpost fight in the direction of Münchengrätz, in which the Austrians were again worsted.

In the First Army the advance on this day was begun by General Von Horn, whose division had held the outposts the night before. At Liebenau Von Horn struck the Austrians, whose force consisted of a small body of infantry, four regiments of cavalry and two batteries of horse artillery. Driven out of the village, and from the field where they next made a stand, the Austrians retreated across the Iser, *via* Turnau, to Podol. The First Army now occupied a position extending through Reichenberg, Gablonz, Liebenau and Turnau; Von Horn's division extending down the Iser from Turnau, with outposts near Podol. Free communication—in fact a junction—was now established with the Army of the Elbe, one division of which occupied Bömisch Aicha.

An attempt made by a company of Prussian riflemen to seize the bridges at Podol, about dusk in the evening, brought on a sharp fight. The forces on each side were reinforced until parts of two Prussian and two Austrian brigades were engaged. A stubborn infantry battle was carried on by moonlight until 1 o'clock in the morning, when the Austrians retreated towards Münchengrätz. By this victory the Prussians secured the passage of the Iser at Podol; the shortest line to Gitschin was opened to them; the communications of Count Clam-Gallas with the main army were threatened; and a plan which he had formed to *riposte* upon the Prussians at Turnau was thwarted.

We will now turn to the Second Army. On this day the Ist Corps concentrated at Liebau and Schomberg, ready to cross the frontier. The Vth Corps was at Reinerz, about twenty miles from the Ist. The Guard Corps, which had just crossed the frontier, in front of Neurode, midway between the two corps, was in a position to support either. The VIth Corps was at Landeck and Glatz, part of its cavalry being sent forward to cover the left of the Vth Corps and maintain communication between the two. After passing the mountains, the entire army, pivoted on Nachod and Skalitz, was to wheel to the left, seize the Josephstadt-Turnau railway, and form a junction along that line with the armies of Frederick Charles.

On the evening of the 26th, the advanced-guard of the Vth Corps occupied Nachod. The distance between the crown prince and Frederick Charles had now been reduced to about fifty miles, while the distance between the extreme corps of the Austrian army was about the same. Von Benedek's strategical advantages were already beginning to disappear. The Prussian demonstrations towards Olmütz had caused the Austrian IId Corps to be retained dangerously far to the right; Count Clam-Gallas was struggling against superior numbers on the Iser, and Von Benedek had only four corps with which he could immediately oppose the four corps of the crown prince.

The Austrian commander ordered the following movements for the next day:

The Xth Corps, from Josephstadt and Schurz, upon Trautenau;

The VIth Corps, from Opocno to Skalitz;

The IVth Corps, from Lanzow to Jaromir;

The VIIIth Corps, from Tynist to beyond Jaromir, to support the VIth;

The IIId Corps, from Königgrätz to Miletin;

The IId Corps, from Senftenberg to Solnitz;

The Reserve Cavalry, from Hohenmauth and Wildenschwerdt to Hohenbrück;

The Light Cavalry to accompany the IId Corps.

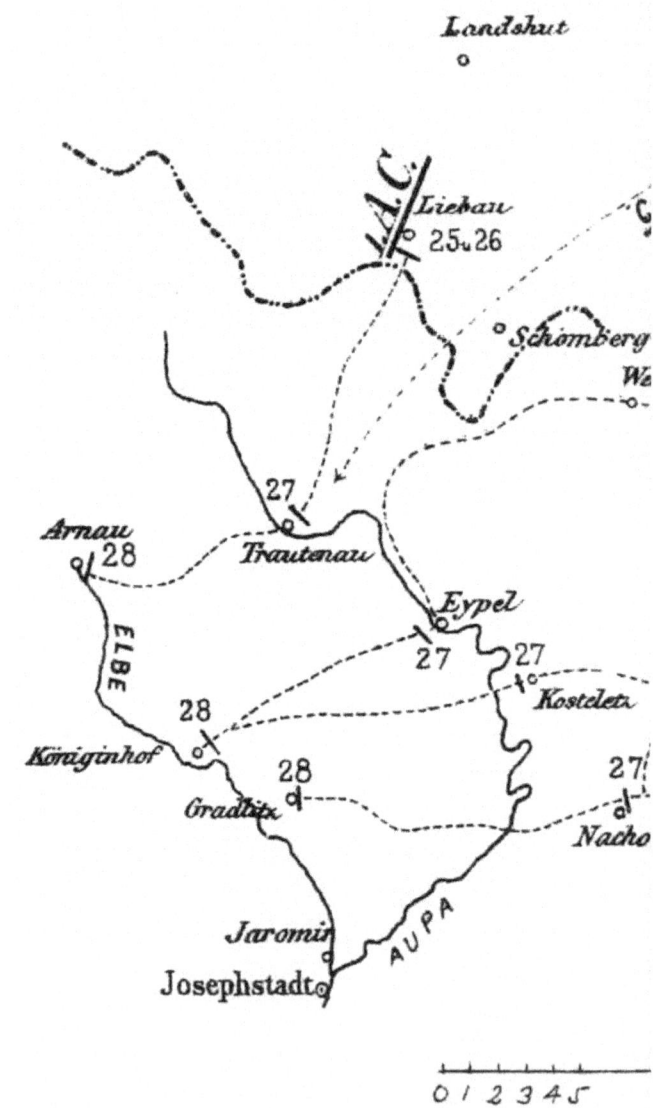

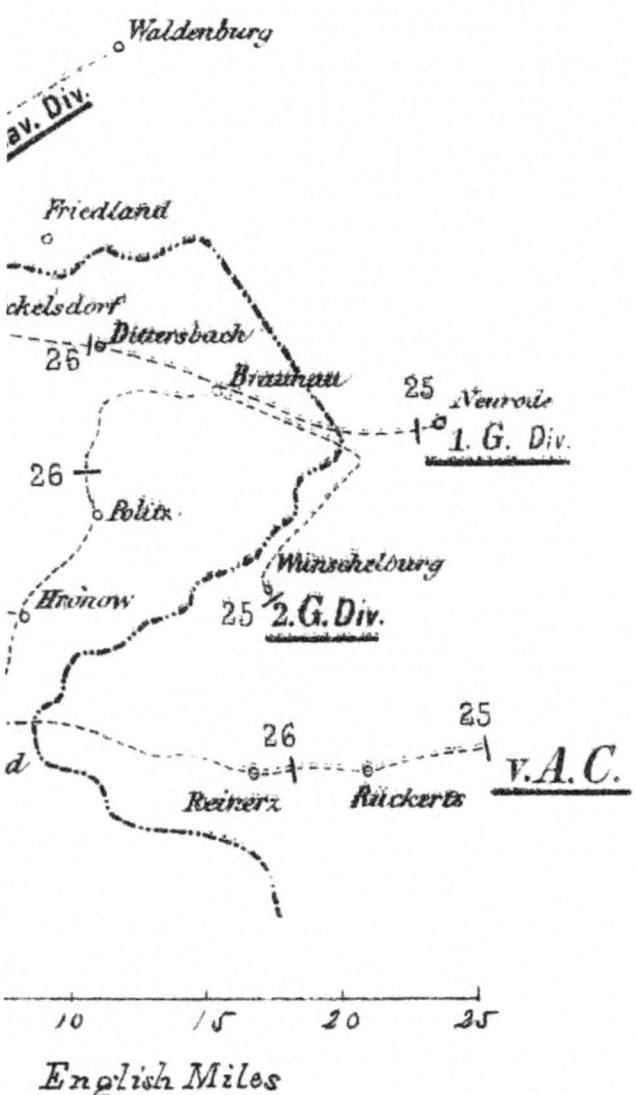

Schweidnitz

Waldenburg

av. Div.

Friedland

ckelsdorf
Dittersbach
26
Braunau

25 Neurode
1. G. Div.

26

Politz

Wünschelburg

Hronow

25 2. G. Div.

26 25

d

Reinerz Rückerts

v. A. C.

10 15 20 25

English Miles

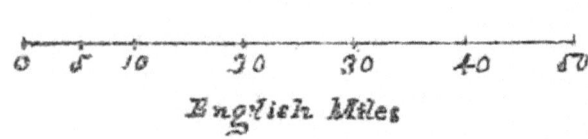

English Miles

Liebau

Waldenburg
C.D.

Schömberg
I

G.C.
Neurode

Trautenau

Wünschelburg
Rückerts
Glat.
V.C.

Königinhof
1.R.C.D.

Skalitz

Jaromir
Josephstadt

Opazu
IV

Sobriç
VI

Königgrätz
Trua

VIII   II   2 L.C.D.

III

Warnberg   Gabel

Giersberg

Parrubitz

Latanischel   3 R.C.D.
C.D.   Aberdort

Politzka

A.R.A.

English Miles

Liebau

Waldenburg
C.D.

1

Schömberg

1

Braunau

Trautenau

G 1.

Politz

2

Mondelz

Königinhof

Reinerz

Glatz

Skalitz

1 R.C.D.

V.

VI.

Lanzow

Jaromir

IV

Josephstadt

Neustadt

Opocno

VI.

Königgrätz

III

Tynist

VIII.

2 L.C.D.

Senftenberg

II

Pardubitz

Wildenschwert

2 R.C.D.

3 R.C.D.

Hohenmauth

Leitomischel

A.R.A.

On the 27th of June the crown prince pushed forward the Ist Corps against Trautenau, and the main body of the Vth Corps upon Nachod. One division of the Guard supported each corps.

The Ist Corps, under Von Bonin, marched in two columns from Liebau and Schomberg, and was to concentrate at Parschnitz, about two miles east of Trautenau, where it was to rest two hours before moving upon the latter place.

Contrary to expectation, the left column arrived first at Parschnitz, the right (with the advanced-guard) being delayed by bad roads. Trautenau was as yet unoccupied by the Austrians; but instead of seizing the town and the heights which overlooked it, on the farther bank of the Aupa River, Von Clausewitz (commanding the left column) obeyed the strict letter of his orders, and waited at Parschnitz two hours, from 8 to 10 a.m., until the advanced guard of the right column arrived.

While Von Clausewitz was thus idly waiting, Mondl's brigade of the Xth Austrian Corps arrived, and took up a strong position in the town and on the heights which commanded it. A stubborn fight took place before the Austrians could be dislodged; and Mondl fell back in good order upon the main body of the Xth Corps, which was hurrying towards Trautenau. Believing himself in complete possession of the field, Von Bonin, at 1 o'clock, declined the assistance of the 1st Division of Guards, which had hurried up to Parschnitz, and the division, after a halt of two hours, marched off to the left, towards Eypel. About half past 3 o'clock the entire Xth Corps, under Von Gablentz, arrived on the field, and made a vigorous attack upon the Prussians. Von Bonin's left wing was turned; and, after fighting six hours, the Prussians were driven from the field, and retreated to the positions from which they had begun their march in the morning.

The Prussian defeat was due to two causes:

1. The delay of Von Clausewitz at Parschnitz, when common sense should have prompted him to exceed his orders, and seize the unoccupied town and heights of Trautenau. For two hours these positions were completely undefended by the Austrians, and could have been occupied by Von Clausewitz without firing a shot. (See Note following).

★★★★★★

Derrécagaix and the Prussian Official History both condemn

Von Clausewitz's delay. Adams, however, finds an excuse for it. He says:

> The first question that arises is, should Clausewitz have occupied Trautenau? Mondl was up, in all probability, and he would have been deeply engaged before Grossmann (commanding the right column) came up, against orders. He could not have been acquainted with the situation, for Bonin himself was not, and it is difficult, therefore, to attach blame to him. The cause of Grossmann's delay is said to have been the hilly character of the road. Mondl, on the other hand, reaching Hohenbrück about 7:30, seems to have halted there to form.
>
> The Austrian official account states that he had occupied the heights since 9:15, and before this he had reached Hohenbrück at 7:45. When he had formed—that is to say, waited to mass his brigade before deploying—the position must have been taken up by him between 8:30 and 9:15. Had Clausewitz advanced, it would have taken three-quarters of an hour to debouch in force south of Trautenau, so that he would have had to continue his march without halting to cross the Aupa, and push forward from Trautenau, contrary to orders, in order to engage Mondl on the very strong ground he by that time had fully occupied.
>
> Probably the latter was informed . . . . that no immediate danger was impending, or he would not have waited leisurely to form. The first duty of the advance, on coming into collision with the enemy, is to occupy rapidly such localities as may prove of use in the impending action.

Nevertheless, the fact remains that the heights were unoccupied when Von Clausewitz arrived at Parschnitz; and it was *his* duty, as well as that of Mondl, on coming into collision with the enemy, to occupy rapidly such localities as might have proved of use in the impending action. As to engaging Mondl "on the very strong ground he by that time had fully occupied," it is sufficient to state that he had only a brigade, while Von Clausewitz had a division. A subordinate commander assumes a grave responsibility when he violates or exceeds his orders; but it is hardly to be expected that an able division commander will fetter himself by observing the strict letter of an order, when he knows, and his superior does not know, that the condition of affairs in his front is such as to offer an opportunity for a successful and valuable stroke, even though that stroke be not contemplated in the orders of his chief. Von Alvensleben understood matters better when he marched without orders to assist Von Fransecky at Königgrätz. If a division commander were never expected to act upon his own responsibility when a movement is urged by his own common sense, it is evident that the position of general of division could be filled by a man of very limited abilities.

★★★★★★

2. The fatuity of Von Bonin in declining the assistance of the Guards. Von Bonin knew that Mondl had not been routed, that he had fallen back "slowly and fighting," and he did not know what other force might be in his immediate front. He had no reason to expect that he would be allowed to pass through the defile without the most stubborn opposition. He knew that he had been opposed by a single brigade, and the plucky resistance of that small force should have made him suspicious that it had stronger forces at its back. His orders were to push on to Arnau, some twelve miles from Trautenau, and to carry out these orders it was necessary to sweep aside the opposition in his front. His declension of assistance when the firing had scarcely ceased, and when the aid of the Guards would have enabled him to clinch his success, was inexcusable. Like Beauregard at Shiloh, Von Bonin seems to have laboured under the delusion that a victory could be sufficiently complete while the enemy's army still remained in his front.

★★★★★★

While this was going on a staff-officer . . . of General Beauregard's headquarters . . . came up to General Bragg and said, 'The General directs that the pursuit be stopped; the victory is sufficiently complete; it is needless to expose our men to the fire of the gun-boats.' General Bragg said, 'My God! was a victory ever sufficiently complete?'—*Battles and Leaders of the Civil War, Vol. I., p. 605*

★★★★★★

The Austrians had certainly gained a brilliant victory. With a force of 33,600 men, they had defeated 35,000 Prussians, armed, too, with breech-loaders, while the victors had only muzzle-loading rifles. The loss of the Prussians was 56 officers and 1,282 men, while the Austrians lost 196 officers and more than 5,000 men. This disparity of loss illustrates the difference in the power of the old and the new rifles; it also speaks volumes for the pluck of the Austrian soldiers.

But the Austrian victory was doomed to be as fruitless as it was costly; for Prussian skill and valour on other fields obliterated all that was gained by Von Gablentz in the bloody combat of Trautenau.

The march of the Vth Corps, under Von Steinmetz, lay through the defile of Nachod, five miles in length, in which the entire corps was obliged to march in a single column. The advanced-guard, which had seized Nachod the night before, pushed forward rapidly, beyond the outlet of the defile, to the junction of the roads leading to Skalitz and Neustadt, where it received orders to halt, and thus cover the issue of the main body through the defile. While the advanced-guard was making preparations for bivouacking, its commander, General Von Loewenfeldt, received news of the approach of the Austrian VIth Corps, which, as we have seen, had been ordered upon Nachod. Hastily forming for action, the Prussian advanced guard received the attack of a brigade, which was reinforced until nearly the whole Austrian corps was engaged. It was a desperate struggle of six and one-half battalions, five squadrons and twelve guns, against twenty-one battalions, eighty guns and a greatly superior force of cavalry.

For three hours the advanced-guard sustained the unequal conflict, with no other reinforcement than Wnuck's cavalry brigade. The Prussian force, in one line 3,000 paces long, without reserves, was sorely pressed, until the main body began to issue from the defile and deploy upon the field. The entire Austrian corps was now engaged. Finally, after a successful charge of Wnuck's cavalry brigade upon the Austrian *cuirassiers*, and the repulse of a heavy infantry attack, Von Steinmetz assumed the offensive, and the Austrians, defeated with great loss, retreated to Skalitz. In the latter part of this action the Prussians were under the immediate command of the crown prince. The Prussian loss was 1,122, killed and wounded; the Austrians lost 7,510, of which number about 2,500 were prisoners.

The 1st Division of the Guards halted this night at Eypel; the 2nd Division at Kosteletz.

This day, which had seen two bloody actions fought by the Second Army, was one of inaction on the part of the armies of Frederick Charles. The day was consumed in constructing bridges across the Iser, at Turnau and Podol, and in concentrating the main body of the army

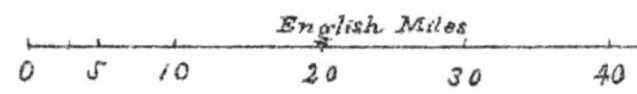

English Miles

0   5   10   20   30   40

Liebau

Schönberg

Arnau

Trautenau

X

Rognitz

Eypel

1.

Kosteleti

G. B

2.

Königinhof

Nachod

Skalitz

VIII

VI.

Miletin

IV

R.C.D.

YI

Habelschwerdt

V

VI.

Horc

Jaromir

Josephstadt

Hohenbruck

Solnitz

3.R.C.D.

2.L.C.D.

Königgrätz

II.

Holic

2.R.C.D.

Pardubitz

Hohenmauth

A.R.A.

Chrast

Nassaberg

A.M.P.

50

on the plateau of Sichrow, preparatory to an attack upon the Austrian position at München grätz.

JUNE 28TH.

The First Army and the Army of the Elbe made a combined attack upon Count Clam-Gallas at Münchengrätz, the Austrians being assailed in front and on both flanks. The Austrian commander had begun his retreat before the Prussian attack commenced; and after a brief resistance, he fell back upon Gitschin, with a loss of about 2,000 men, killed, wounded and prisoners. The Prussian loss was only 341. The armies of Frederick Charles were now completely united. One division was pushed forward to Rowensko, and the remaining eight, numbering, with the cavalry, upwards of 100,000 men, were concentrated upon an area of about twenty square miles. Some distress began to be felt because of the short supply of food and the difficulty of getting water; for only part of the provision trains had come up, and the Austrian inhabitants, when they abandoned their homes, had filled up the wells. Two roads led east from the Prussian position; one *via* Podkost, and the other *via* Fürstenbrück, but both united at Sobotka. The Austrian rear guard was driven from Podkost during the night, and both roads were open for the Prussian advance on the following morning.

Frederick Charles has been severely (and it would seem justly) criticised for his inaction on the 27th of June. His explicit instructions from Von Moltke should have been enough to cause him to hasten forward, and so threaten the Austrian left as to relieve the pressure on the crown prince. And there was another reason for prompt action. As already mentioned, the victory of Podol had opened to Frederick Charles the shortest line to Gitschin, from which place he was now distant only fifteen miles, while Clam-Gallas, at Münchengrätz, was twenty miles away from the same point. The town of Gitschin, like Ivrea in 1800, or Sombref and Quatre-Bras in 1815, had accidentally become a strategic point of the first importance by reason of the relative positions of the opposing armies and the direction of the roads necessary for the concentration of each. All the roads leading from the Iser, from Turnau to Jung Bunzlau, centre at Gitschin, whence other roads branch out to Neu Bidsow, Königgrätz, Josephstadt, Königinhof, and other important points.

The possession of Gitschin by either army would seriously delay, and perhaps eventually prevent, the concentration of the other. A prompt movement to Gitschin by Frederick Charles would have cut off Clam-Gallas, who could then have effected a junction with Von Benedek only by a circuitous march of such length as to make it probable that his two corps would have been eliminated altogether from the problem solved on the field of Königgrätz. As the Austro-Saxons at Münchengrätz, covering the roads to Prague, could have protected their communications with that city, while menacing the communications of the Prussians with their base, it was, doubtless, necessary to dislodge them from that position; but Frederick Charles might have promptly pushed to Gitschin a force sufficient to seize and hold the place, and still have kept in hand enough troops to defeat Clam-Gallas so heavily as to drive him back in complete rout; for Frederick Charles' force numbered, at this time, nearly 140,000 men, while Clam-Gallas had not more than 60,000.

This movement would not have really divided Frederick Charles' army, for the force at Gitschin and the one attacking at Münchengrätz would have been practically within supporting distance, and in direct and unimpeded communication with each other. Moreover, the nearest troops available to oppose such a force thrust forward to Gitschin would have been the single Austrian Corps (the IIId) which was at Miletin, quite as far from Gitschin as the main body of Frederick Charles' army would have been. Frederick Charles' entire army could have been at Gitschin quite as soon as Von Benedek could have sent thither any force large enough to offer respectable opposition; and the necessity of hurrying troops to that point would have caused the Austrian commander to relax materially the pressure upon the crown prince; a pressure which Frederick Charles had every reason to believe greater than it really was. Hozier states that the Prussian commander had formed a plan to capture the entire army of Clam-Gallas; but Adams truly remarks that the destruction of the Austro-Saxons at Münchengrätz would not have compensated for a severe defeat of the crown prince.

Moreover, as we have seen, Clam-Gallas was not captured but fell back upon Gitschin, whence he was able to form a junction with the main army. Had Frederick Charles pushed a force to Gitschin, and with the rest of his army dealt Clam-Gallas such a blow as to send him reeling back towards Prague, the Prussian general would have reaped the double advantage of interposing between the divided forces of the enemy, and facilitating his own junction with the crown prince. Adams correctly says of Frederick Charles:

The fault attributable to the prince is, that with a superiority of force at his command, which gave him unbounded advantage over his enemy, he refused to incur risks which that fact reduced to a minimum, in the general interests of the campaign. (See note following).

★★★★★★

Note: The above criticism on the delay of Frederick Charles is based mainly on the comments of Major Adams, in his *Great Campaigns in Europe*. Hozier, who, in the main, follows the Prussian Staff History of the war, has nothing but praise for the prince. The absence of adverse criticism on the action of Frederick Charles in the Prussian Official History is, perhaps, explained by the high military and social position of that general. Adams seems to think that a forward movement by Frederick Charles would have caused Clam-Gallas to abandon München-grätz at once, and does not seem to consider that if the Austro-Saxons had not been dislodged, Clam-Gallas would have had the Prussian communications by the throat, while covering his own, and that this advantage might have compensated him for his separation from Von Benedek.

It may be urged in objection to these comments, that Frederick Charles did not know the exact condition of affairs in his front at the time. To this it may be replied that ability to appreciate a strategical advantage, and power to form a correct estimate of the enemy's dispositions, are a test of a general's merits as a strategist. McClellan is not excused for believing that, when Lee was attacking his right at Gaines' Mill, the enemy was in strong force between the Federal army and Richmond; and Hamley is not gentle in his comments on Napoleon's failure to estimate correctly the force and dispositions of the Prussians at Jena; though, being an Englishman, he does not hesitate to adopt another standard of criticism when he finds it necessary to defend Wellington for his error in leaving at Hal 17,000 men so sorely needed at Waterloo.—(See Hamley's *Operations of War*).

★★★★★★

To return to the Second Army:

The crown prince received information, at 1 o'clock in the morning, of the defeat of the Ist Corps at Trautenau.

The 1st Division of the Guards was at once ordered to move against Von Gablentz from Eypel, and the 2nd Division (which had been intended to support the Vth Corps) was ordered from Kosteletz to support the 1st Division. The movement was begun at 4 a. m. Anticipating the attack, Von Gablentz took up a position facing east, with his left in Trautenau and his right at Prausnitz, about five miles south of the former village. A brigade of the Austrian IVth Corps, ordered to his assistance from Jaromir, mistook the route, and did not arrive in time to participate in the action.

The Prussian attack was begun by the 1st Division of the Guards at 9:30 a.m. The Austrian centre and right were forced back upon Soor and Altenbach. The brigade on the Austrian left was contained by two Prussian battalions until the arrival of the 2nd Division, at 12:30 p. m., when it was driven back upon Trautenau, and the greater part of it captured. The main body of the Austrians was driven from the field, and retreated upon Neustadt and Neuschloss. The Prussian loss was 713, killed and wounded; the Austrian loss 3,674, killed, wounded and prisoners.

While the Guards were thus engaged in repairing the defeat of the Ist Corps, the Vth Corps was battling with the Austrians at Skalitz. Baron Ramming, commanding the Austrian VIth Corps, having called for reinforcements, Von Benedek ordered the VIIIth Corps to Dolan, about four miles west of Skalitz, and gave the command of both corps to the Archduke Leopold. Early on the morning of the 28th the VIIIth Corps relieved the VIth in its position on the east bank of the Aupa, in front of Skalitz, and the latter took up a position as a reserve in rear of the right wing. The IVth Corps was stationed at Dolan.

On the Prussian side, Von Steinmetz had been reinforced by a brigade of the VIth Corps. The Austrians had begun a retrograde movement before the Prussian attack commenced; and the corps of Baron Ramming was already too far to the rear to give efficient support to the VIIIth Corps. After a severe action, the Austrians were driven from their position, and retreated upon Lanzow and Salney; the IVth Corps, as a rear guard, holding Dolan. The Prussian loss in the Battle of Skalitz was 1,365 killed, wounded and missing; the Austrians lost nearly 6,000 men, of whom 2,500 were prisoners.

The Battles of Soor and Skalitz opened the passes of Trautenau and Nachod to the unimpeded advance of the Ist and VIth Corps. During these battles the crown prince was stationed at Kosteletz, from which point he might easily reach either battlefield, if his presence should become necessary. In the night he went to Trautenau.

The distance between the advanced guard of Frederick Charles, at Ztowa, and that of the crown prince, at Burkersdorf (near Soor), was only twenty-seven miles.

Grüssau

Liebau ☒ G.D.

Schömberg

nelbe

Trautenau

Arnau ☒ G

Eypel

☐ Neuschloss

X

Königinhof

Nachod

Rückerts

1 R.C.D. Skalita ☒ VI.

Filetin

IV ☐ ☒ V.

☐ Lannow

Dolan ☒ VI

III ☐

Jaromir

VI. ☐

☐ VIII

Salney

Josephstadt

Holohlaw

III ☒ 2 L.C.D.

☒ Smirzitz

2. R.C.D.

☒ 3 R.C.D.

Königgratz

Holic

☒ A.R.A.

Pardubitz

☒ A.M.P.

Intelligence received at the Prussian headquarters of the battles in which the armies had been engaged, rendered it certain that of the seven Austrian army corps, the IVth, VIth, VIIIth and Xth were opposed to the crown prince, and that only the Ist Corps and the Saxons were arrayed against Frederick Charles. The position of the IIId Corps was unknown; but it was clear that it was the only one that could come to the assistance of Count Clam-Gallas, as the IId Corps was known to be far to the rear. The necessity of relieving the crown prince from the overwhelming numbers of Von Benedek, and the prospect of being able to deliver a crushing blow upon the inferior force in his front, alike rendered it of the utmost importance that Frederick Charles should move promptly upon Gitschin. (It should be remembered that, in addition to the four corps immediately opposed to the crown prince, the IIId and IId Austrian Corps were at Von Benedek's disposal; the latter being scarcely more than two marches distant from Josephstadt).

Apparently impatient at the prince's delay, Von Moltke reiterated the instructions already given him, saying, in a telegram from Berlin on June 29th:

His Majesty expects that a speedy advance of the First Army will disengage the Second Army, which, notwithstanding a series of successful actions, is still momentarily in a precarious situation.

Frederick Charles, who had already decided to advance without further delay, at once moved as follows:

The Left, from Turnau, *via* Rowensko;

The Centre, from Podol, *via* Sabotka;

The Right, from Münchengrätz, *via* Ober Bautzen and Sabotka;

The Army of the Elbe, from Münchengrätz, *via* Unter Bautzen and Libau.

The advance of the army was rendered difficult by the small number of roads available. The leading divisions were started as early as possible, to make a long march, in order that the other divisions might march in the evening on the same roads. It was, even then, necessary for the Army of the Elbe to make a long detour.

Count Clam-Gallas, having been promised the assistance of the

IIId Corps, resolved to make a stand near Gitschin. His position was on a range of hills west and north of that village, his right resting upon the village of Eisenstadt, his left on the Anna Berg, near Lochow. In front of the centre were the rocky heights of Prywicin, which, being almost impassable for ordinary pedestrians, would isolate the attacks of the enemy, while, terminating in front of the Austrian position, they could not interfere with the free movements of the troops on the defensive. In front of the hills were ravines, gullies and broken ground. The position was thus very strong for an army whose *rôle* was a purely defensive one.

Von Tümpling's division, (5th) leaving Rowensko at 1:30 p.m., came in contact with the enemy shortly after 3 o'clock. Von Werder's division (3rd) left Zehrow at noon; but, having a greater distance to march, did not strike the enemy until 5:30. Von Tümpling immediately attacked the Austrian right, with a view to cutting off Count Clam-Gallas from the main army of Von Benedek. The action continued, with varying fortune, until 7:30, when, Von Tümpling having carried the village of Dielitz, in the centre of the Austrian right wing, Von Werder having gained ground on the left, and Von Benedek having sent word that the assistance of the IIId Corps could not be given, Count Clam-Gallas ordered a retreat.

The Austrians retired in good order upon Gitschin; the retreat of the right wing being covered by an attack of a brigade upon the Prussians at Dielitz; that of the left by an attack of a regiment of infantry and a battalion of rifles. Both attacks were repulsed with heavy loss. Following the enemy, the Prussians, after a sharp fight with the Austrian rear guard in the streets, occupied Gitschin after midnight. The Prussian loss was 2,612 killed, wounded and missing; the Austrians lost about 7,000 men, of whom 4,000 were prisoners. Count Clam-Gallas reported to Von Benedek that he had been defeated, that he was no longer able to oppose Frederick Charles, and that he was retreating upon Königgrätz.

Von Benedek now determined to throw his main force on Frederick Charles, leaving a containing force to oppose the crown prince. But with this object in view, his dispositions were faulty. Strangely ignoring the results of the Battles of Nachod, Soor and Skalitz, he seems to have thought that one corps would suffice to hold the crown prince in check; and on the morning of the 29th he issued orders for the advance of the IIId Corps to Gitschin and the Reserve Cavalry to Horzitz. The IId, VIth, VIIIth and Xth were to follow on the next

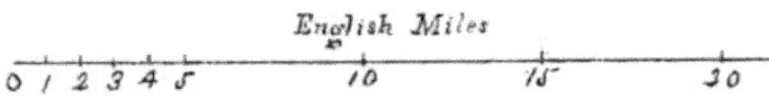

day in the direction of Lomnitz and Turnau. But during the day events occurred which necessitated a complete change of plan.

In the Second Army the Ist Corps marched *via* Trautenau to Pilnikau, and the cavalry division following it halted at Kaile, where the crown prince established his headquarters.

The Guards advanced upon Königinhof, from which place they drove out a brigade of the Austrian IVth Corps, capturing about 400 prisoners.

The Vth Corps (with one brigade of the VIth) marching upon Gradlitz, encountered the other brigades of the Austrian IVth Corps at Schweinschädel, and after an action of three hours, drove them from the field with a loss of nearly 5,000 men, killed, wounded and prisoners. The Austrians retreated to Salney. The crown prince had now reached the Elbe.

During the day Von Benedek, becoming alarmed at the progress of the Second Army, countermanded the order for the IIId Corps to move upon Gitschin, and directed it to remain at Miletin. The Ist Corps and the Saxons were ordered to join the main army *via* Horzitz and Miletin; but the orders, as we have seen, came too late to save them from their defeat at Gitschin. The rest of the army was concentrated before night upon the plateau of Dubenetz, against the army of the crown prince, as follows:

> The IVth Corps at Salney, with the 1st Reserve Cavalry Division, and the 2nd Light Cavalry Division on its right and rear;
>
> The IId Corps at Kukus, on left of IVth;
>
> The VIIIth Corps near Kasow (one brigade in line on left of IId Corps, the other brigades as reserve);
>
> The VIth Corps on the left of the VIIIth;
>
> The 3rd Reserve Cavalry Division on the left of the VIth Corps;
>
> The 2nd Reserve Cavalry Division on the extreme left wing;
>
> The Xth Corps, in reserve, between Stern and Liebthal.

Five army corps and four cavalry divisions were thus concentrated on a line five and one-half miles long. The nature of the ground was unfavourable to the interior communications of the line, but it was, in the main, a strong position, with the Elbe on its front, and the fortress of Josephstadt protecting its right flank.

The junction of the Prussian Armies now seemed assured, and the strategical situation was decidedly against Von Benedek. His great fault was his failure to decide promptly in regard to the army which he should contain while throwing his weight upon the other. Placing an exaggerated value upon his interior position, he does not seem to have considered that every hour of Prussian advance diminished his advantages; and he was, apparently, unable to make his choice of the two plans of operations which presented themselves. His best move, if made in time, would have been against Frederick Charles. True, his communications could have been quickly cut, in this case, by a successful advance of the Second Army across the Elbe; while in moving against the crown prince, his communications could not so readily have been seized by Frederick Charles.

But, on the other hand, topographical features made it an easier matter to contain the Second Army than the First Army and the Army of the Elbe. If the Austrian field marshal had learned the lesson taught at Atlanta, Franklin and Petersburg, he would have made use of hasty entrenchments. The Xth Corps and VIth Corps, strongly entrenched, could certainly have held the passes against the assaults of the crown prince. The ground was admirably adapted to defence, and the entrenchments would have more than neutralized the superiority of the needle gun over the Lorenz rifle. To have invested and reduced the entrenched camps, if possible at all, would have required much more time than Von Benedek would have needed for disposing of Frederick Charles.

To have advanced by the road leading to Olmütz or Bömisch Trübau, the crown prince would have been compelled to mask the passes with at least as many troops as garrisoned the camps at their outlets, or his own communications would have been at the mercy of the Austrians. This would have left him only two corps; and an invasion of Moravia with this small force, every step of the advance carrying him farther away from Frederick Charles, would have been an act of suicidal madness, which he would not have seriously contemplated for a moment. When Osman Pasha, eleven years later, paralyzed the advance of 110,000 Russians, by placing 40,000 Turks in a hastily entrenched position on their right, at Plevna, he showed plainly how Von Benedek might have baulked the Second Army with entrenched positions at the Silesian passes.

Leaving, then, two corps to take care of the crown prince, the Austrian commander would have had (including the Saxons) six corps, and nearly all of the reserve cavalry and artillery, to use against Frederick Charles. Count Clam-Gallas, instead of undertaking the task of holding the line of the Iser, should have destroyed the bridges; and opposing the Prussians with a strong rear-guard at the different crossings, obstructing the roads, offering just enough resistance to compel his adversary to deploy and thus lose time, but avoiding anything like a serious action, he should have fallen back *via* Gitschin to form a junction with Von Benedek. He could thus have gained sufficient time for his chief to arrive at Gitschin as soon as Frederick Charles; and the army of the latter, numbering not more than 130,000 men, would have been opposed by an army of fully 200,000 Austrians. (At the Battle of Königgrätz, Frederick Charles had 123,918 men. His losses at Gitschin aggregated 2,612 men. It seems, therefore, that 130,000 men is a high estimate of the maximum force which he would have been able to oppose to Von Benedek at Gitschin, had the latter made a junction with Clam-Gallas at that point).

What the result would have been we can best judge from the course of the Battle of Königgrätz before the crown prince arrived upon the field.

Hozier, Adams, Derrécagaix and (above all) the Prussian Official History of the Campaign of 1866, claim that the best move of Von Benedek would have been against the crown prince. If we consider the successful passage of the defiles by the Second Army as a thing to be taken for granted in Von Benedek's plan of campaign, there can be no doubt that the Austrian commander should have turned his attention to the crown prince, and that he should have attacked him with six corps, as soon as the Prussians debouched from the defiles of Trautenau and Nachod. The line of action here suggested as one that would probably have resulted in Austrian success, is based entirely on the condition that the Second Army should be contained at the defiles, by a force strongly entrenched after the American manner of 1864-5; a condition not considered by the eminent authorities mentioned above. After the crown prince had safely passed the defiles, Von Benedek had either to attack him or fall back. The time for a successful move against Frederick Charles had passed.

Von Benedek had carefully planned an invasion of Prussia. Had he been able to carry the war into that country, his operations might, perhaps, have been admirable; but when the superior preparation of the Prussians enabled them to take the initiative, he seems to have been incapable of throwing aside his old plans and promptly adopting new ones suited to the altered condition of affairs. Von Benedek was a good tactician and a stubborn fighter; but when he told the emperor

"Your Majesty, I am no strategist," and wished to decline the command of the army, he showed a power of correct self-analysis equal to that displayed by Burnside when he expressed an opinion of his own unfitness for the command of the Army of the Potomac. The brave old soldier did not seem to appreciate the strategical situation, and was apparently losing his head. (See note following).

★★★★★★

Col. C. B. Brackenbury, R. A., who accompanied the Austrian headquarters during the campaign, says that on one occasion he heard Von Benedek say, hotly, to his disputing staff, "For God's sake do something!" and mentions the following incident:

"After the Battles of Nachod and Trautenau the second officer of the Intelligence Department examined all the prisoners, and obtained clear information of the whereabouts of all the columns of the crown prince, then struggling through the mountain passes. He wrote his report and took it to the officer who had been sent to Benedek to decide the strategy of the campaign. At that time several Austrian corps were close by.

"The general looked at the paper and had all the facts explained to him. He then dismissed the captain, who, however, remained and said, probably in that tone of distrust which prevailed, 'Now, Herr General, I have shown you that the crown prince can be beaten in detail if attacked by our great force within half a day's march; may I ask what you propose to do with the Austrian army?' The general replied, 'I shall send it against Prince Frederick Charles.' The captain put his hands together in an attitude of supplication and said, 'For God's sake, sir, do not,' but was ordered out of the room. I did not know this fact when Benedek said, the day after the defeat of Königgrätz, 'Did you ever see such a fine army so thrown away?'"—*Field Works*, by Col. C. B. Brackenbury, R. A.

★★★★★★

With all the advantages of interior lines, he had everywhere opposed the Prussians with inferior numbers; he had allowed the Crown prince to pass through the defiles of the mountains before he opposed him at all; six of his eight corps had suffered defeat; he had lost more than 30,000 men; and now he was in a purely defensive position, and one which left open the road from Arnau to Gitschin for the junction of the Prussian Armies.

It would have been better than this had the Austrians everywhere fallen back without firing a shot, even at the expense of opposing no obstacles to the Prussian concentration; for they could then, at least, have concentrated their own army for a decisive battle without the demoralisation attendant upon repeated defeats.

JUNE 30TH.

A detachment of cavalry, sent by Frederick Charles towards Arnau, met the advanced-guard of the 1st Corps at that place. Communication was thus opened between the two armies.

It was evident that the advance of Frederick Charles would, by threatening the left and rear of the Austrians, cause them to abandon their position on the Elbe, and thus loosening Von Benedek's hold on the passages of the river, permit the crown prince to cross without opposition.

The following orders were therefore sent by Von Moltke:

> The Second Army will hold its ground on the Upper Elbe; its right wing will be prepared to effect a junction with the left wing of the First Army, by way of Königinhof, as the latter advances. The First Army will press on towards Königgrätz without delay.
>
> Any forces of the enemy that may be on the right flank of this advance will be attacked by General Von Herwarth, and separated from the enemy's main force.

On this day the armies of Frederick Charles marched as follows:

> The IIId Corps, to Aulibitz and Chotec;
>
> The IVth Corps, to Konetzchlum and Milicowes;
>
> The IId Corps, to Gitschin and Podhrad;
>
> The Cavalry Corps, to Dworetz and Robaus;
> The Army of the Elbe, to the vicinity of Libau;
>
> The Landwehr Guard Division, which had been pushed forward from Saxony, arrived at Jung Buntzlau.

★★★★★★

Gitschin, Jung Buntzlau, and Libau are shown on the earlier map of the evening of 28th June. The positions of the other places here mentioned are, in reference to Gitschin, as follows: Aulibitz, nearly 4 miles east; Chotec, about 7½ miles east; Konetzchlum, about 6½ miles east-south-east; Milicowes, about 4½ miles south-south-east; Podhrad, about 2 miles southwest; Robaus, about 2 miles east; Dworetz, near, and north of, Robaus.

★★★★★★

The Second Army remained in the position of the preceding day.

Von Benedek's army remained in its position on the plateau of Dubenetz.

JULY 1ST.

At 1 o'clock in the morning Von Benedek began his retreat towards Königgrätz.

The IIId Corps moved to Sadowa;

The Xth Corps, to Lipa;

The 3rd Reserve Cavalry Division, to Dohalica;

The VIth Corps, to Wsestar;

The 2nd Reserve Cavalry Division, to a position between Wsestar and Königgrätz;

The VIIIth Corps, to Nedelist, on left of the village;

The IVth Corps, to Nedelist, on right of the village;

The IId Corps, to Trotina;

The 2nd Light Cavalry Division, to the right of the IId Corps;

The 1st Reserve Cavalry Division, behind Trotina;

The 1st Corps took up a position in front of Königgrätz;

The 1st Light Cavalry Division, on the left of the 1st Corps;

The Saxons were stationed at Neu Prim.

The Prussian Armies, though at liberty to concentrate, remained separated for tactical considerations. The armies were to make their junction, if possible, upon the field of battle, in a combined front and flank attack upon the enemy. In the meantime, as they were only a short day's march from each other, the danger to be apprehended from separation was reduced to a minimum.

Frederick Charles' armies moved as follows:

The IIId Corps, to Miletin and Dobes;

The IVth Corps, to Horzitz and Gutwasser;

The IId Corps, to Aujezd and Wostromer;

The 1st Cavalry Division, to Baschnitz;

POSITION OF BOTH ARMIES
On the evening of the 2nd July, 1866.

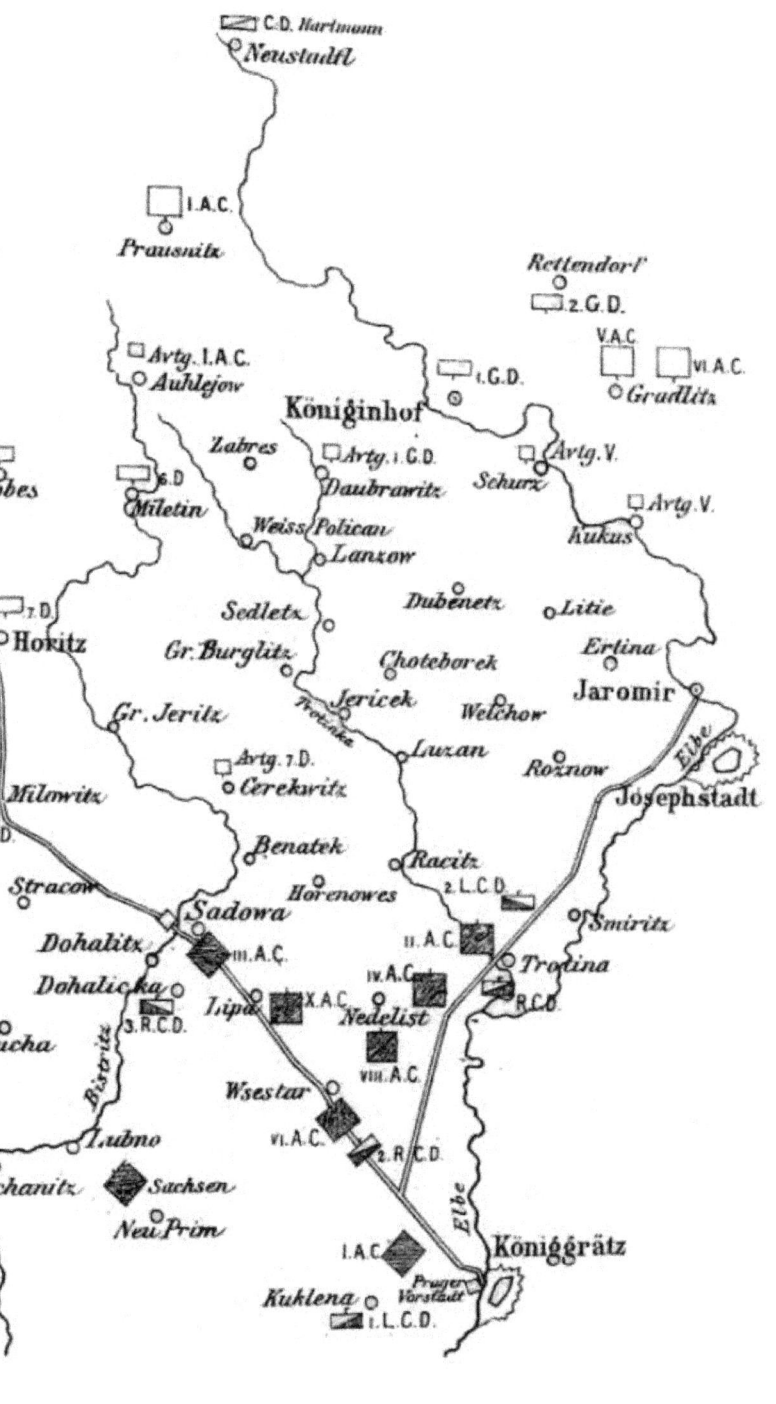

The 2nd Cavalry Division, to Liskowitz;

The Army of the Elbe, to a position between Libau and Hochwesely.

In the Second Army, the Ist Corps was thrown across the Elbe to Prausnitz, and the VIth Corps arrived at Gradlitz.

July 2nd.

The Army of the Elbe moved forward to Chotetitz, Lhota and Hochweseley, with an advanced-guard at Smidar.

The Guard Landwehr Division advanced to Kopidlno, a few miles west of Hochweseley.

The Austrians remained in the positions of the preceding day, but sent their train to the left bank of the Elbe.

Incredible as it seems, the Prussians were ignorant of the withdrawal of the Austrians from the plateau of Dubenetz, and did not, in fact, even know that Von Benedek had occupied that position. The Austrians were supposed to be behind the Elbe, between Josephstadt and Königgrätz. On the other hand, Von Benedek seems to have been completely in the dark in regard to the movements of the Prussians. The Prussian Staff History acknowledges that:

> The outposts of both armies faced each other on this day within a distance of four and one-half miles, without either army suspecting the near and concentrated presence of the other one.

Each commander ignorant of the presence, almost within cannon shot, of an enormous hostile army! Such a blunder during our Civil War would, probably, have furnished European military critics with a text for a sermon on the mob-like character of American armies.

Supposing the Austrians to be between Josephstadt and Königgrätz, two plans were open to Von Moltke's choice.

First: To attack the Austrian position in front with the First Army and the Army of the Elbe, and on its right with the Second Army. This would have necessitated forcing the passage of a river in the face of a formidable enemy; but this passage would have been facilitated by the flank attack of the crown prince, whose entire army (except the Ist Corps) was across the river. It would have been a repetition of Magenta on a gigantic scale, with the crown prince playing the part of McMahon, and Frederick Charles enacting the *rôle* of the French emperor.

Second: To manoeuvre the enemy out of his position by moving upon Pardubitz; the occupation of which place would be a serious menace to his communications. The latter movement would necessitate the transfer of the Second Army to the right bank of the Elbe, and then the execution of a flank march in dangerous proximity to the enemy; but its successful execution might have produced decisive results. This movement by the right would have been strikingly similar to Von Moltke's movement by the left, across the Moselle, four years later. The resulting battle might have been an antedated Gravelotte, and Von Benedek might have found a Metz in Königgrätz or Josephstadt. At the very least, the Austrians would, probably, have been manoeuvred out of their position behind the Elbe.

Before determining upon a plan of operations, it was decided to reconnoitre the Elbe and the Aupa. The Army of the Elbe was directed to watch the country towards Prague, and to seize the passages of the river at Pardubitz. The First Army was ordered to take up the line Neu Bidsow-Horzitz and to send a detachment from its left wing to Sadowa, to reconnoitre the line of the Elbe between Königgrätz and Josephstadt. The Ist Corps was to observe the latter fortress, and to cover the flank march of the Second Army, if the movement in question should be decided upon. The remaining corps of the Second Army were, for the present, to remain in their positions, merely reconnoitring towards the Aupa and the Metau.

These orders were destined to be speedily countermanded.

Colonel Von Zychlinsky, who commanded an outpost at the castle of Cerakwitz, reported an Austrian encampment near Lipa, and scouting parties, which were then sent out, returned, after a vigorous pursuit by the Austrian cavalry, and reported the presence of the Austrian army in force, behind the Bistritz, extending from Problus to the village of Benatek. These reports, received after 6 o'clock p. m., entirely changed the aspect of matters.

Under the influence of his war experience, Frederick Charles was rapidly developing the qualities of a great commander; his self-confidence was increasing; and his actions now displayed the vigour and military perspicacity of Mars-la-Tour, rather than the hesitation of Münchengrätz.

★★★★★★

It is interesting to note the growth of great generals under the influence of their actual experience in war. The Frederick of Rossbach and Leuthen was very different from the Frederick of Mollwitz. In 1796 we find Napoleon calling a council of war before hazarding a second attempt upon Colli's position at St. Michel, and showing, even in that vigorous and brilliant campaign, a hesitation never shown by the Napoleon of Ulm and Austerlitz. The Grant of Vicksburg was not the Grant of Shiloh; and Lee at Chancellorsville and Petersburg does not seem like the same commander who conducted the impotent campaign of 1861 in West Virginia. The old saying, "*Great generals are born, not made,*" is not altogether true. It would be more correct to say, "*Great generals are born, and then made.*"

★★★★★★

He believed that Von Benedek, with at least four corps, was about to attack him; but he unhesitatingly decided to preserve the advantages of the initiative, by himself attacking the Austrians in front, in the early morning, while the Army of the Elbe should attack their left. The co-operation of the crown prince was counted upon to turn the Austrian right, and thus secure victory.

With these objects in view, the following movements were promptly ordered:

The 8th Division to be in position at Milowitz at 2 a. m.;

The 7th Division to take post at Cerakwitz by 2 a. m.;

The 5th and 6th Divisions to start at 1:30 a. m., and take post as reserves south of Horzitz, the 5th west, and the 6th east, of the Königgrätz road;

The 3rd Division to Psanek, and the 4th to Bristan; both to be in position by 2 a. m.

The Cavalry Corps to be saddled by daybreak, and await orders;

The reserve Artillery to Horzitz;

General Herwarth Von Bittenfeld, with all available troops of the Army of the Elbe, to Nechanitz, as soon as possible.

Lieutenant Von Normand was sent to the crown prince with a request that he take post with one or two corps in front of Josephstadt, and march with another to Gross Burglitz.

The chief-of-staff of the First Army, General Von Voigts-Rhetz, hastened to report the situation of matters to the king, who had assumed command of the armies on June 30th, and now had his headquarters at Gitschin. The measures taken by Frederick Charles were approved, and Von Moltke at once issued orders for the advance of the entire Second Army, as requested by that commander. These orders were sent at midnight; one copy being sent through Frederick Charles at Kamenitz; the other being carried by Count Finkenstein direct to the crown prince at Königinhof. The officer who had been sent by Frederick Charles to the crown prince was returning, with an answer that the orders from army headquarters made it impossible to support the First Army with more than the Ist Corps and the Reserve Cavalry. Fortunately, he met Finkenstein a short distance from Königinhof. Comparing notes, the two officers returned together to the crown prince, who at once issued orders for the movement of his entire army to the assistance of Frederick Charles.

In order to deliver his dispatches to the crown prince, Finkenstein had ridden twenty-two and one-half miles, over a strange road, on a dark, rainy night. Had he lost his way; had his horse suffered injury; had he encountered an Austrian patrol, the history of Germany might have been different. It is almost incredible that the Prussian general should have diverged so widely from the characteristic German prudence as to make success contingent upon the life of an *aide-de-camp*, or possibly the life of a horse. Even had the other courier, riding *via* Kamenitz, reached his destination safely, the time that must have elapsed between the crown prince's declension of co-operation and his later promise to co-operate, would have been sufficient to derange, and perhaps destroy, the combinations of Von Moltke.

Let us now examine the Austrian position. Derrécagaix describes it as follows:

> In front of the position, on the west, ran the Bistritz, a little river difficult to cross in ordinary weather, and then very much swollen by the recent rains.
> On the north, between the Bistritz and the Trotina, was a space of about five kilometres, by which the columns of the assailant might advance. Between these two rivers and the Elbe the ground is broken with low hills, covered with villages and woods, which gave the defence advantageous points of support. In the centre the hill of Chlum formed the key of the position, and commanded the road from Sadowa to Königgrätz. The heights of Horenowes covered the right on the north. The heights of Problus and Hradek constituted a solid support for the left. At the south the position of Liebau afforded protection on this side to the communications of the army. (See note following).

The position selected had, then, considerable defensive value; but it had the defect of having at its back the Elbe and the defiles formed by the bridges.

★★★★★★

Note: The author's own observations of the topography of the field correspond, in the main, with the description given above. The Bistritz, however, is not such a formidable obstacle as one might infer from the description quoted. At the village of Sadowa it is a mere ditch, not much larger than some of the *acequias* in Colorado or Utah. It is perhaps eight feet wide and three feet in depth. It could hardly have been an obstacle to infantry. Its muddy bottom and marshy banks doubtless rendered it a considerable obstacle for artillery, but the eight villages through which it flows, within the limits of the battle field, certainly could have furnished abundant material for any number of small bridges required for crossing it. In the vicinity of Nechanitz, the Bistritz, having received the waters of a tributary creek, becomes a true obstacle, as it spreads out to a width of about thirty yards, and the banks are swampy. It should be remarked that at the time of the author's visit to Königgrätz, there had been very heavy rains, and the condition of the stream was probably the same as on the day of the battle.

★★★★★★

On this subject, however, Hozier says:

> The Austrian commander took the precaution to throw bridges over the river. With plenty of bridges, a river in rear of a position became an advantage. After the retreating army had withdrawn across the stream, the bridges were broken, and the river became an obstacle to the pursuit. Special, as well as general, conditions also came into play. . . . The heavy guns of the fortress scoured the banks of the river, both up and down stream, and, with superior weight of metal and length of range, were able to cover the passage of the Austrians.

In considering the Austrian retreat, we shall find that neither of these distinguished authorities is entirely right, or wholly wrong, in regard to the defects and advantages of the position described.

The following dispositions were ordered by Von Benedek:

> The Saxons to occupy the heights of Popowitz, the left wing slightly refused, and covered by the Saxon Cavalry;

The 1st Light Cavalry Division, to the rear and left, at Problus and Prim;

The Xth Corps on the right of the Saxons;

The IIId Corps to occupy the heights of Lipa and Chlum, on the right of the Xth Corps;

The VIIIth Corps in reserve, in rear of the Saxons.

In case the attack should be confined to the left wing, the other corps were merely to hold themselves in readiness. If, however, the attack should extend to the centre and right, the following dispositions were to be made:

The IVth Corps to move up on the right of the IIId to the heights of Chlum and Nedelist;

The IId Corps, on the right of the IVth, constituting the extreme right flank;

The 2nd Light Cavalry Division, to the rear of Nedelist;

The VIth Corps to be massed on the heights of Wsestar;

The Ist Corps to be massed at Rosnitz;

The 1st and 3rd Cavalry Divisions to take position at Sweti;

The 2nd Reserve Cavalry Division, at Briza;

The Reserve Artillery behind the Ist and VIth Corps.

The Ist and VIth Corps, the five cavalry divisions and the Reserve Artillery were to constitute the general reserve.

A slight attempt was made to strengthen the position by throwing up entrenchments. Six batteries were constructed on the right, as well as breastworks for about eight companies of supporting infantry. The infantry breastworks, as well as the batteries, were constructed by engineer soldiers, and were of strong profile, with traverses, and had a command of eight feet. There was not the slightest attempt to have the infantry shelter themselves with hasty entrenchments. Even the earthworks that were constructed were of no use; for a misunderstanding of orders caused the line of battle to be established far in advance of them. On the left but little was done to strengthen the position before the Prussian attack began.

The Battle of Königgrätz, July 33rd.

Notwithstanding the heavy rain, the muddy roads, and the late hour at which the orders had been received, the divisions of the First

Army were all at their appointed places soon after dawn. The Army of the Elbe pushed forward energetically, and at 5:45 o'clock its commander notified Frederick Charles that he would be at Nechanitz between 7 and 9 o'clock, with thirty-six battalions. The First Army was at once ordered forward.

The 8th Division marched on the left of the high road, as the advanced-guard of the troops moving upon Sadowa.

The 4th and 3rd Divisions marched on the right of the road, abreast of the 8th.

The 5th and 6th Divisions followed the 8th on the right and left of the road respectively, while the Reserve Artillery followed on the road itself.

The Cavalry Corps had started from Gutwasser at 5 o'clock, and it now marched behind the right wing to maintain communication with the Army of the Elbe.

The 7th Division was to leave Cerekwitz as soon as the noise of the opening battle was heard, and was to join in the action according to circumstances.

The divisional cavalry of the 5th and 6th Divisions was formed into a brigade, and a brigade of the cavalry division was attached to the IId Corps.

About 7:30 the advanced-guard of the Army of the Elbe reached Nechanitz, where it encountered a Saxon outpost, which retired after destroying the bridges.

About the same time the 8th Division advanced in line of battle upon Sadowa. The Austrian artillery opened fire as soon as the Prussians came in sight. The latter took up a position near the Sadowa brickfield, and skirmishing began.

The 4th Division took up a position at Mzan, on the right of the 8th, and its batteries engaged in combat with the Austrian artillery.

The 3rd Division formed on the right of the 4th, near Zawadilka.

The 5th and 6th Divisions formed line at Klenitz; one on each side of the road.

The Reserve Cavalry was stationed at Sucha.

At the first sound of the cannon Von Fransecky opened fire upon the village of Benatek, which was soon set on fire by the Prussian shells. The village was then carried by assault by the advanced-guard of the 7th Division.

There was now a heavy cannonade all along the line. The heavy downpour of the last night had given place to a dense fog and a drizzling rain; and the obscurity was heightened by the clouds of smoke which rose from the guns. Frederick Charles rode along the right wing, giving orders to respond to the Austrian batteries by firing slowly, and forbidding the crossing of the Bistritz. His object was merely to contain Von Benedek, while waiting for the weather to clear up, and for the turning armies to gain time.

At 8 o'clock loud cheering announced the arrival of the King of Prussia upon the battle field. As soon as Frederick Charles reported to him the condition of affairs, the King ordered an advance upon the line of the Bistritz. The object of this movement was to gain good points of support for the divisions upon the left bank of the Bistritz, from which they might launch forth, at the proper time, upon the main position of the enemy. The divisions were cautioned not to advance too far beyond the stream, nor up to the opposite heights.

The Austrian position differed slightly from the one ordered on the eve of the battle. The Saxons, instead of holding the heights eastward of Popowitz and Tresowitz, found a more advantageous position on the heights between Problus and Prim, with a brigade holding the hills behind Lubno, Popowitz and Tresowitz. Nechanitz was held merely as an outpost. The remaining dispositions of the centre and left were, on the whole, as ordered the night before; on the right they differed materially from the positions designated.

Instead of the line Chlum-Nedelist, the IVth Corps took up its position on the line Cistowes-Maslowed-Horenowes, 2,000 paces in advance of the batteries that had been thrown up.

The IId Corps formed on the right of the IVth, on the heights of Maslowed-Horenowes.

The Ist and VIth Corps and the Cavalry took their appointed positions, and the Reserve Artillery was stationed on the heights of Wsestar and Sweti.

In the language of the Prussian Staff History:

"Instead of the semi-circle originally intended, the Austrian line of battle now formed only a very gentle curve, the length of which, from Ober-Prim to Horenowes, was about six and three-fourths miles, on which four and three-fourths *corps d'armee* were drawn up. The left wing had a reserve of three weak brigades behind it, and on the right wing only one brigade covered the ground between the right flank and the Elbe. On the other hand, a main reserve of two corps of infantry and five cavalry divisions stood ready for action fully two miles behind the centre of the whole line of battle."

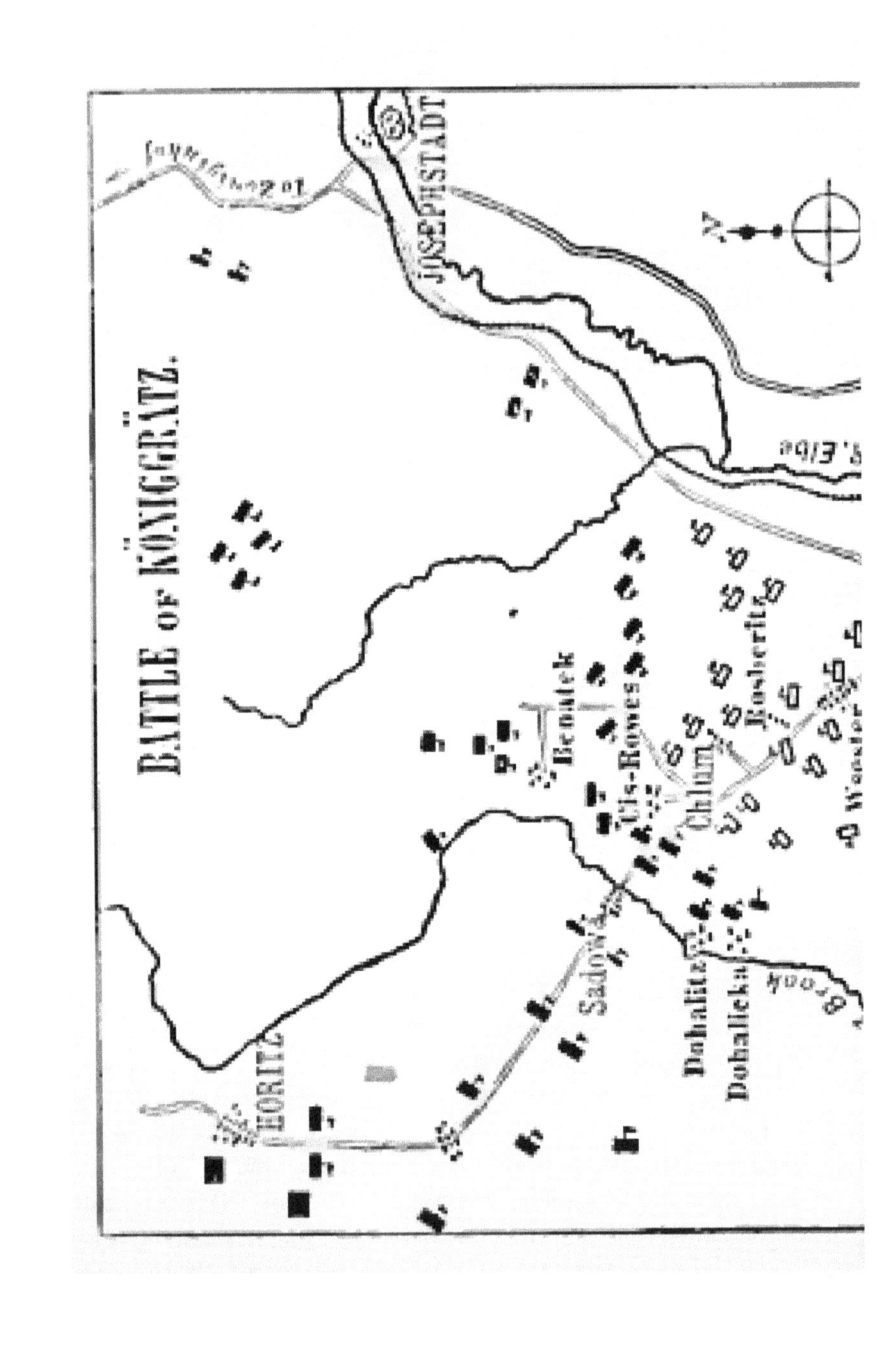

BATTLE OF KÖNIGGRÄTZ.

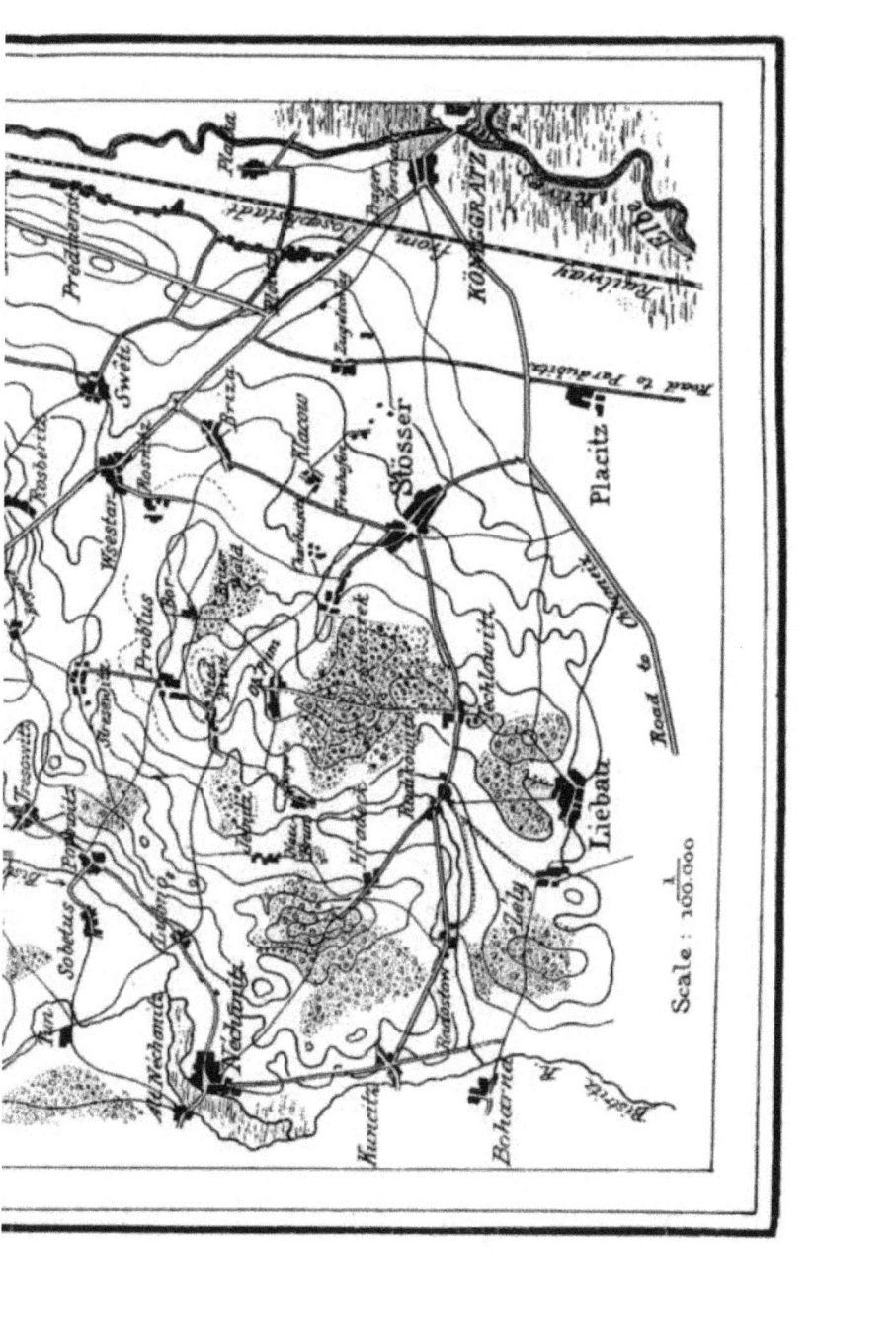

Scale : $\frac{1}{100,000}$

The strength of the Austrian Army was 206,100 men and 770 guns. At this period of the battle it was opposed by a Prussian army of 123,918 men, with 444 guns. The arrival of the Second Army would, however, increase this force to 220,984 men and 792 guns.

The 7th Division, which had already occupied the village of Benatek, was the first to come into serious conflict with the Austrians. The attack, beginning thus on the left, was successively taken up by the 8th, 4th and 3rd Divisions; and the advanced-guard of the Army of the Elbe being engaged at the same time, the roar of battle extended along the entire line.

In front of the 7th Division were the wooded heights of Maslowed, known also as the Swiep Wald. This forest, extending about 2,000 paces from east to west, and about 1,200 from north to south, covered a steep ridge intersected on its northern slope by ravines, but falling off more gradually towards the Bistritz. Against this formidable position Von Fransecky sent four battalions, which encountered two Austrian battalions, and, after a severe struggle, drove them from the wood.

Now was the time to break the Austrian line between Maslowed and Cistowes, and, turning upon either point, or both, roll up the flanks of the broken line. The advanced battalions were quickly reinforced by the rest of the division; but all attempts to *débouche* from the wood were baffled. Heavy reinforcements were drawn from the Austrian IVth and IId Corps, and a furious counter-attack was made upon the Prussians. Calling for assistance, Von Fransecky was reinforced by two battalions of the 8th Division; but he was still struggling against appalling odds. With fourteen battalions and twenty-four guns, he was contending against an Austrian force of forty battalions and 128 guns. Falling back slowly, contesting the ground inch by inch, the Prussian division, after a fierce struggle of three hours, still clung stubbornly to the northern portion of the wood. Still the Austrians had here a reserve of eleven battalions and twenty-four guns, which might have been hurled with decisive effect upon the exhausted Prussians, had not other events interfered.

As soon as the 7th Division had advanced beyond Benatek, the 8th Division advanced against the woods of Skalka and Sadowa. Two bridges were thrown across the Bistritz, west of the Skalka wood, by the side of two permanent bridges, which the Austrians had neglected to destroy. The reserve divisions (5th and 6th) advanced, at the same time, to Sowetitz, and the Reserve Artillery to the Roskosberg. As soon as the 8th Division crossed the Bistritz, it was to establish communication with the 7th Division, and turn towards the Königgrätz highroad. The woods of Skalka and Sadowa were occupied without much difficulty; the Austrian brigade which occupied them falling back in good order to the heights of Lipa, where the other brigades of the IIId Austrian Corps were stationed. On these heights, between Lipa and Langenhof, 160 guns were concentrated in a great battery, which sent such a "hailstorm of shells" upon the advancing Prussians as to check effectually all attempts to *débouche* from the forests.

The 4th Division advanced from Mzan, and the 3rd from Zawadilka, soon after the 8th Division moved forward. The retreat of the Austrian brigade from Sadowa had uncovered the flank of the outposts, and compelled the withdrawal of the troops successively from Dohalitz, Dohalica and Mokrowous to the main position westward of Langenhof and Stresetitz, and these outposts were consequently gained by the Prussians with slight loss. Further advance of the 4th and 3rd Divisions was, however, prevented by the rapid and accurate fire of the Austrian batteries.

The advanced-guard of the Army of the Elbe had gained the left bank of the Bistritz, part of the left wing crossing by the bridge of Nechanitz (which had been repaired with gates and barn doors) and part by wading breast-deep across the stream. The right wing of the advanced-guard was obliged to march down stream to Kuncitz, where it crossed, after dislodging a small force of Saxons and repairing the bridge. The Saxon outposts were all driven back to the main position, and the Prussian advanced-guard occupied the line Hradek-Lubno, thus covering the crossing of the main body. The Prussians succeeded in throwing only one bridge at this part of the field; and as the entire Army of the Elbe was obliged to cross upon it and defile through Nechanitz, the deployment was necessarily slow.

At 11 o'clock the Prussian advance had been checked. The Army of the Elbe was slowly forming in rear of the line Hradek-Lubno. The First Army, advancing, as we have seen, by echelon of divisions from the left, had gained the position Maslowed-Sadowa Wood-Mokrowous, thus executing a wheel of about an eighth of a circle to the right. The immediate object of the advance had been practically gained, it is true, by the occupation of the line of the Bistritz, and the conversion of the strong advanced posts of the Austrians into good points of support for the Prussians. Yet Fransecky was sorely pushed on the left, and the 8th Division was suffering so severely from the fire of the Austrian guns, that Frederick Charles deemed it necessary to order the 5th and 6th

Divisions to move up to the Sadowa wood. All attempts of these fresh troops to gain ground towards the heights of Lipa were repulsed, and the Prussian advance again came to a standstill. A counter-attack by a single Austrian brigade against the Sadowa wood (made without Von Benedek's permission) was repulsed.

The position of the First Army was now critical. The last battalion of the infantry reserves had been brought into action. Von Fransecky was on a desperate defensive. The other divisions were all subjected to a furious, crushing fire from nearly 250 pieces of artillery, which the Austrians had brought into action on the heights from Lipa to Problus; while, owing partly to the wooded ground, partly to the difficulty of crossing the stream, and partly to the inefficiency of the Prussian artillery officers, only 42 guns were on the left bank of the Bistritz to reply to this formidable cannonade. Only a portion of Frederick Charles' guns were brought into action at all; and their long range fire from the positions west of the Bistritz was ignored by the Austrian batteries, whose entire energy was devoted to a merciless pelting of the Prussian infantry.

The statement of the Prussian Staff History that the centre was in no danger, seems, therefore, to savour more of patriotism than of candour. To advance was impossible. The infantry was suffering terribly from the Austrian fire; the artillery was feebly handled; and the cavalry could render no assistance. There was danger that the army would be shaken to pieces by Von Benedek's artillery, and that the demoralized troops would then be swept from the field by the comparatively fresh infantry and cavalry of the Austrians. The king and his generals eagerly scanned the northern horizon with their glasses; and, with the intense anxiety of Wellington at Waterloo, waited for tidings from, the army on the left, and strained their vision for a sight of the advancing columns. The question of retreat was discussed. The Reserve Cavalry was ordered up to Sadowa, apparently with a view to covering the withdrawal of the army to the right bank of the stream. It was now past 1 o'clock. It was resolved to hold the line of the Bistritz at all hazards, and a heavy artillery fire was kept up. In the meantime, events on other parts of the field were already beginning to extricate the First Army from its perilous situation.

At 11:30, the 14th and 15th Divisions of the Army of the Elbe having come upon the field, an attack was ordered upon both flanks of the Saxons. The 15th Division, followed by a brigade of cavalry, moved, through Hradek, against Ober-Prim. The 14th Division moved on the heights east of Popowitz, through the forest, against Problus. The advanced-guard, between the two divisions, moved to the attack, pushing its flanks forward, for the double purpose of avoiding the heavy fire from the enemy's front and masking the movements of the turning divisions. The Prince of Saxony, believing it a favourable opportunity to assume the offensive, attacked the Prussian advanced-guard with a Saxon brigade. The attack, though made with great spirit, was repulsed. Again the prince attacked, this time with two brigades; but the advancing Saxons being struck on the left flank by the 15th Division, were driven back with heavy loss, and Ober-Prim was carried by the Prussians. General Herwarth Von Bittenfeld had succeeded in bringing 66 guns to the left bank of the Bistritz, and he now pushed them forward to within 2,000 paces of Nieder Prim, upon which they concentrated a heavy fire, under cover of which the place was carried by a regiment of the 15th Division. The 14th Division, having gained possession of Popowitz and the wood east of that village, now joined the 15th Division in a concentric attack upon Problus.

The Prince of Saxony had not only observed the preparations for this attack, but he had also observed the arrival of the Prussian Second Army at Chlum; and he now, at 3 o'clock, ordered a retreat to the heights southwest of Rosnitz. The troops at Problus, acting as a rearguard, offered a stubborn resistance to the advancing Prussians; but they were driven from the village, and the advance of the 14th and 15th Divisions was checked only by the artillery fire of the Saxons and the VIIIth Corps, stationed on the hills north-east of Problus.

During this time the Second Army had been working great results. At 8 o'clock Von Alvensleben, commanding the advanced-guard of the Guard Corps, at Daubrowitz, heard the cannonade in the direction of Benatek. Without waiting for orders, he at once put his command in march for the scene of conflict, notifying his corps commander of his departure, and sending word to Von Fransecky that he would be at Jericek by 11:30. The rest of the corps quickly followed, marching straight across country, uphill and downhill, pushing through the heavy mud with such restless energy that several of the artillery horses dropped dead from fatigue. The advanced-guard arrived at Jericek at 11 o'clock, and at the same hour the heads of the columns of the main body arrived at Choteborek, to which point the crown prince had hurried in advance of the troops.

The VIth Corps advanced from its position, near Gradlitz, in two columns. The 12th Division marched, *via* Kukus and Ertina, to the heights east of Rosnow, detaching a battalion and a squadron to mask the fortress of Josephstadt. The 11th Division marched, *via* Schurz, to Welchow. As soon as it neared the latter place Von Mutius, commanding the corps, ordered both divisions to keep connection and march to the sound of the cannonade. The troops pushed on "over hills, meadows and ditches, through copses and hedgerows," across the swampy valley of the Trotina, part of the troops crossing the stream by the single bridge, and part wading breast-deep through the water. At 11 o'clock the 11th Division arrived at the heights north of Racitz, and came under the fire of the enemy's batteries.

At 8 o'clock the Vth Corps began its march, *via* Schurz and Dubenitz, to Choteborek; and at 11 o'clock its advanced-guard was approaching that village.

The Ist Corps did not start until 9:30. It marched *via* Zabres, Gross-Trotin and Weiss Polikau; and at 11 o'clock it had not yet reached Gross-Burglitz.

Thus, at 11 o'clock, the only troops that had reached the Trotina were the Guards and the VIth Corps; and they were still two and one-half miles from the left wing of the First Army. In three hours the Second Army had been so concentrated as to reduce its front from twenty-two and one-half miles to nine miles; and it now occupied the line Burglitz-Jericek-Choteborek-Welchow.

The crown prince, from his station on the heights of Choteborek, about four and one-half miles from Maslowed, had an extended view towards the valley of the Bistritz; and notwithstanding the rain and fog, he could trace the direction of the contending lines by the smoke of the burning villages and flashes of the guns. It was evident that his columns were marching in such a direction as to bring them directly upon the flank and rear of the Austrian troops already engaged; but, though the formidable heights of Horenowes appeared to be occupied by only one battery, it seemed probable that the passage of the Elbe by the crown prince was known by Von Benedek, and that the troops on the Austrian right were waiting behind the crest of the hills, to spring forward into action when the Prussians should undertake to cross the swampy valley between the Trotina and the heights of Horenowes. The different divisions were ordered to direct their march upon a prominent group of trees on the Horenowes hill.

The Austrians were now in a position of extreme danger. The heights of Horenowes, which seemed to offer such a formidable obstacle to the advance of the crown prince, had been left almost defenceless. As we have seen, the Austrian IVth and IId Corps had taken up the line Cistowes-Maslowed-Horenowes, and the space between the right flank and the Elbe was guarded by only one brigade and two battalions. To make matters worse, the IVth and IId Corps had been drawn into the fight with Von Fransecky in the Swiep Wald, and, facing west, they now presented a flank to the advancing columns of the crown prince. The advance of these two corps beyond the line Chlum-Nedelist had carried them far beyond support; and now, with the Prussian Second Army within two and one-half miles of them, their reserves were fully three miles away.

Von Benedek discovering that these two corps had not taken up their designated positions, sent orders, before 11 o'clock, to their commanders, to fall back to the positions originally assigned to them. Unfortunately, the commander of the IVth Corps, ignorant of the approach of the crown prince, and flushed with his success against Von Fransecky, thought it an opportune moment to assume a vigorous offensive against the Prussian left, and would not make the movement ordered until he had sent a report to that effect to his chief. The projected offensive was disapproved, and the former order was repeated. The two corps now retired to the positions originally designated, the movement being covered by the fire of 64 pieces of artillery posted on the plateau of Nedelist.

The withdrawal had been delayed too long; for the crown prince already had 48 guns in position between Racitz and Horenowes, the Prussian infantry was advancing, and the Austrian movement partook, consequently, of the nature of a retreat. Yet it is greatly to the credit of the Austrian troops that they were able to execute a flank movement—and a retrograde movement, too—under the fire of the enemy; though they had been in action fully three hours.

At noon Von Benedek received a telegram from Salney, *via* Josephstadt, announcing the approach of the Second Army. At this very moment the guns of the crown prince were playing upon the Austrian right flank.

The advanced-guard of the 1st Division of Guards had debouched from Zizilowes at 11:15 a.m.; its right flank being covered by the cavalry brigade which had covered the left of the 7th Division. The advanced-guard of the 2nd Guard Division, (which had been separated from the main body by the Reserve Artillery of the 1st Division cutting into the column on the road) without waiting for the arrival of its comrades, joined the 1st Division in its attack upon Horenowes. At noon the 12th Division had captured the Horicka Berg, the 11th Division had driven the Austrians from Racitz, and the Guards were advancing upon Horenowes. The withdrawal of the Austrian IId Corps had been covered by 40 guns posted east of Horenowes, which kept up a heavy fire upon the Prussians. But the Guards easily carried Horenowes, the position of the great battery was turned, the hostile infantry was advancing upon its flank, and the artillery was forced to retire.

The 12th Division, in the meantime, had captured Sendrasitz, cutting off the Austrian brigade which had been covering the right flank. The 11th Division then moved up to a position north of Sendrasitz, on the left of the Guards, and the latter advanced to Maslowed. The Prussians now had 90 guns on the heights of Horenowes; and most of these pieces were hurried forward beyond Maslowed, within 1,300 paces of the Austrian position, where they prepared the way for the infantry assault by a vigorous cannonade.

When the Guards advanced, the Austrian IVth Corps was still engaged in taking up its new position. Unchecked by the fire of more than 100 guns in position west of Nedelist, the Guards crushed the two battalions on the left of the IVth Corps, and penetrated into the gap; the left wing rolling up the flank of an Austrian brigade, and pushing on in the direction of Sweti; while the right wing, changing front to the right, stormed the village of Chlum, which, though the key of the Austrian position, was occupied by only a single battalion. As the Guards advanced, the force under Von Alvensleben, which had constituted the advanced-guard in the morning, moved forward in echelon on their right. A brigade of the Austrian IVth Corps, which, by some mistake, had been left at Cistowes, and was now marching to the new position of its corps, was struck by Von Alvensleben, and driven to the westward of Chlum with heavy loss. Simultaneously with the Guards, the VIth Corps advanced upon the enemy, the 11th Division capturing Nedelist, and the 12th driving the cut-off Austrian brigade into Lochenitz.

The Austrians made several determined attacks from Langenhof and the Lipa wood upon the Prussians in Chlum; but though they fought with great bravery and penetrated into the village, they were repulsed by the Guards, who then seized Rosberitz and the forest of Lipa. The 1st Austrian Reserve Cavalry Division, consisting of five regiments, charged the Prussians south of Chlum. The brigade on the left consisted of two regiments of *cuirassiers*, and was formed in double column: the one on the right was composed of two regiments (one of *cuirassiers* and one of lancers), formed in double column, with a regiment of *cuirassiers* following as a second line. The charge was repulsed by four companies of the infantry of the Guard. It is remarkable that in this case, the cavalry came within 200 yards of the infantry before the latter opened fire.

At 3 o'clock matters had, consequently, changed very much for the worse with the Austrians. On the left, the Saxons had been driven from their position; on the right, the Prussian Guards and VIth Corps occupied the line Rosberitz-Nedelist-Lochenitz. The Austrian IVth and IId Corps had been defeated, and were retreating upon Wsestar, Sweti, Predmeritz and Lochenitz. The 1st Division of the Guards had captured 55 guns, and had seized the key of the Austrian position. The Austrian IIId Corps was sandwiched between the Guards and the First Army. Yet the position of the Guards was full of danger. In the valley of Sweti-Wsestar-Rosnitz were the two intact corps of Austrian reserves, with more than 70 squadrons of cavalry; and between Wsestar and Langenhof were massed the powerful batteries of the reserve artillery, which kept Rosberitz and Chlum under a heavy fire. The main body of the 2nd Division of the Guards was just ascending the heights of Maslowed. There were no other troops within a mile and a quarter upon whom they could depend for assistance.

Von Benedek, who had taken his position between Lipa and Chlum, hearing of the occupation of the latter village by the Prussians, could scarcely believe the surprising news. As he rode hurriedly toward Chlum, the information was rudely corroborated by a volley from the Prussians, which mortally wounded an *aide-de-camp*, and seriously injured several other members of his escort. There was no longer any doubt. Victory was now out of the question, and it was necessary to take prompt measures to save the right wing from annihilation, and to prevent the retreat of the rest of the army from being cut off.

A brigade of the Austrian Ist Corps was sent to reinforce the Saxons near Problus, and another brigade of the same corps was sent against the Lipa wood and the heights west of Chlum. The latter brigade, reinforced by a brigade of the IIId Corps and fragments of the IVth Corps, made three desperate attacks upon the advanced-guard of the 2nd Division and part of the 1st Division of the Prussian Guards at these points, only to recoil, completely baffled, before the deadly fire of the needle gun. The IIId Corps no longer had any intact troops; it was between two fires; it began its retreat, and abandoned the village of Lipa to the Prussians. On the left, the main body of the 1st Division of the Guards was engaged at Rosberitz with the Austrian VIth Corps. Advancing resolutely to the attack, the Austrians dislodged the Guards from the village after a bloody struggle; but as they halted at the outskirts of the town to re-form for another assault, the Guards were reinforced by the advanced-guard of the Ist Corps.

At the same time, the commander of the Prussian VIth Corps, leaving the 12th Division engaged with the Austrians at Lochenitz, half-wheeled the 11th Division to the right, and advanced from Nedelist upon Rosberitz. The Austrian IId Corps was already in retreat. A counter-attack of the Guards and the Ist Corps drove the Austrians out of Rosberitz; and the 11th Division striking them on the flank routed them with heavy loss. The 11th Division then attacked a brigade of the Austrian IVth Corps, which had taken up a position near Sweti to protect the reserve artillery. The brigade and the artillery were driven back to the village, which was carried by assault, many cannon being captured. The Vth Corps reached Horenowes at 4 o'clock, and was designated as the general reserve of the army.

The full tide of Prussian success had now set in. The 16th Division had not yet crossed at Nechanitz, but the 14th and 15th Divisions had defeated the Saxons and the Austrian VIIIth Corps, and the allies were in retreat. Both of the Austrian flanks had been crushed, and the First Army was now actively engaged in an attack upon Von Benedek's front.

The *aide-de-camp* sent by the crown prince to announce his approach had been delayed by the condition of the roads and the necessity of making a long detour, and did not arrive at the royal headquarters until late in the afternoon. The crown prince's advance was first made known to the commander of the First Army by the flashes of the Prussian guns on the heights of Horenowes. Soon after, the Prussian columns were seen ascending the heights of Maslowed. The fire of the Austrian guns in front perceptibly diminished, and it was evident that some of the batteries had changed front to the right.

It was clear that the Second Army had struck the Austrian flank; and at 3:30 o'clock the king ordered "an advance all along the line" of the First Army. The retreat of the Austrian Xth Corps had begun, but it was concealed by the nature of the ground, and covered by the line of artillery, which devotedly maintained its position, and kept up a heavy fire, until its own existence was imperilled by the advance of the foe. The Xth Corps had passed well beyond the danger of infantry pursuit when the advance of the First Army was ordered. The Austrian artillerists held to their position until the enemy was almost at the muzzle of the cannon, and then withdrawing to Rosnitz and Briza, with all the guns that their stubborn defence had not compelled them to sacrifice, again opened fire upon the Prussians.

The cavalry, too, devoted itself to the task of covering the retreat. The Prussian cavalry, which had been delayed by the blocking of the bridges by the artillery, and the crowding of the roads by the infantry, now appeared in the front of the pursuers, and fierce cavalry combats took place near Langenhof, Stresetitz and Problus. Though eventually overmatched, the Austrian cavalry made a noble fight, and, at the sacrifice of its best blood, materially assisted in covering the retreat of the army.

Frederick Charles, bringing up 54 guns to the heights of Wsestar and Sweti, opened fire upon the new line of Austrian artillery. The Austrian batteries replied with spirit, until the advance of the 11th Division upon Rosnitz and Briza compelled them to withdraw, with the loss of 36 guns. Still undaunted, the artillery took up a new position on the line Stösser-Freihofen-Zeigelshag. Here all available guns were brought into action, and under their fire the Prussian pursuit virtually ended. Withdrawing in excellent order to the line Placitz-Kuklena, the Austrian artillery kept up a duel with the Prussian guns on the line Klacow-Stezerek until long after darkness had set in.

The Prussian Staff History says:

> The behaviour of the cavalry and the well-sustained fire of the powerful line of artillery at Placitz and Kuklena, proved that part, at least of the hostile army still retained its full power of resistance.
>
> It is true that affairs behind this line of artillery bore a very different aspect. At first the corps had, for the most part, taken the direction of the bridges northward of Königgrätz, but were prevented from using them by the advance of the Prussian extreme left wing. This caused the different bodies of troops to become promiscuously and confusedly mingled together. The flying cavalry, shells bursting on all sides, still further increased the confusion, which reached its climax when the commandant of Königgrätz closed the gates of the fortress.
>
> Hundreds of wagons, either overturned or thrust off from the highroad, riderless horses and confused crowds of men trying

to escape across the inundated environs of the fortress and the river, many of them up to their necks in water—this spectacle of wildest flight and utter rout, immediately before the gates of Königgrätz, was naturally hidden from the view of the pursuing enemy.

A prompt pursuit would, however, have been impracticable, even if the Prussians had fully appreciated the extent of the Austrian demoralization. The concentric attacks, so magnificently decisive on the field, had produced an almost chaotic confusion on the part of the victors themselves. Owing to the direction of their attacks, the Second Army and the Army of the Elbe were "telescoped" together; and the advance of the First Army had jammed it into the right flank of the former and the left flank of the latter. At noon the front of the combined Prussian armies had been more than sixteen miles long. The front of this great host was now but little more than two miles; and men of different regiments, brigades, divisions, corps, and even armies, were now indiscriminately mingled together.

Aside from this confusion, the exhaustion of the Prussian soldiers precluded pursuit. Most of them had left their bivouacs long before dawn, and it had been a day of hard marching and hard fighting for all. Many had been entirely without food, all were suffering from extreme fatigue, and several officers had fallen dead on the field from sheer exhaustion.

As a result of the exhaustion of the Prussians and the excellent conduct of the Austrian cavalry and artillery, Von Benedek slipped across the Elbe, and gained such a start on his adversaries that for three days the Prussians lost all touch with him, and were in complete ignorance of the direction of his retreat.

Thus ended the great Battle of Königgrätz. The Prussian losses were 9,153, killed, wounded and missing. The Austrians lost 44,200, killed, wounded and missing, including in the last classification 19,800 prisoners. They also lost 161 guns, five stands of colours, several thousand muskets, several hundred wagons and a pontoon train. The sum total of the killed, wounded and missing (exclusive of prisoners) in this battle was 27,656.

It is not necessary, for the present, even to sketch the retreat of the Austrian Army upon Olmütz and Vienna; the masterly march of Von Moltke to the Danube; the Italian disasters of Custozza and Lissa; and the campaign in which the Army of the Maine defeated the Bavarians and the VIIIth Federal Corps. (A sketch of these operations is given in the appendices). Königgrätz was the decisive battle of the war. Austria could not rally from her disaster, and twenty-three days after the battle the truce of Nikolsburg virtually ended the contest.

COMMENTS.

It is not only on account of its great and far-reaching results that Königgrätz must be rated as one of the greatest battles of the world. In point of numbers engaged, it was the greatest battle of modern times; for the two contending armies aggregated nearly half a million men. In this respect it exceeded Gravelotte, dwarfed Solferino and even surpassed the "Battle of Nations" fought on the plains of Leipsic, fifty-two years before.

Yet, considering the numbers engaged, the loss of life was not great. The sum total of the killed and wounded was nearly 6,000 less than at Gettysburg, though in that sanguinary struggle the combined strength of the Union and Confederate armies was less than that of the Austrian Army alone at Königgrätz. (See note following).

★★★★★★

The strength of the Union Army at Gettysburg was 78,043. The Confederate Army numbered about 70,000. The Union Army lost 3,072 killed, and 14,497 wounded. The Confederates lost 2,592 killed, and 12,709 wounded. In comparing the losses of Gettysburg with those of Königgrätz, no account is here taken of the "missing" in either the Union or the Confederate losses; though the missing (exclusive of prisoners) are figured in with the killed and wounded of the Prussian and Austrian Armies. The figures in regard to Gettysburg are taken from the tables (compiled from official records) in *Battles and Leaders of the Civil War*. The figures in regard to Königgrätz are taken from the Prussian Official History.

★★★★★★

In fact, of all the battles of the War of Secession, Fredericksburg, Chattanooga and Cold Harbor were the only ones in which the losses of the *victors*, in killed and wounded, did not exceed, in proportion to the numbers engaged, the losses of the *defeated* army at Königgrätz. A bit of reflection upon these facts might convince certain European critics that the failure of victorious American Armies to pursue their opponents vigorously was due to other causes than inefficient organisation or a lack of military skill. In the words of Colonel Chesney:

In order to pursue, there must be someone to run away; and, to the credit of the Americans, the ordinary conditions of European warfare in this respect were usually absent from the great battles fought across the Atlantic. Hence, partly, the frequent repetition of the struggle, almost on the same ground, of which the last campaign of Grant and Lee is the crowning example.

It is, perhaps, not too much to say, that had Von Benedek been a Lee, and had his army been of the nature of Lee's army, even if defeated at Königgrätz, the next day would have found him on the left bank of the Elbe, under the shelter of hasty entrenchments presenting a bold front to the Prussians; for there was no reason, aside from demoralization, for the retreat of the Austrians far from the scene of their defeat. Their communications were neither intercepted nor seriously endangered; their losses had not been excessive; and, but for their discouragement and loss of *morale*, there is no reason why their defeat at Königgrätz should have been decisive.

Not the least of the causes of the Austrian defeat was the autocratic policy of Von Benedek, which caused the entire management of the army to be centralised in his own person, and the plan of battle to be locked up in his own mind. However brave, willing and obedient a subordinate officer may be, there can be no doubt that his duties will be better done, because more intelligently done, if he has a clear knowledge of the part that he is called upon to perform. The higher the rank, and the more important the command, of the subordinate officer, the more certainly is this the case. Yet Von Benedek seems to have desired from his corps commanders nothing more than the blind obedience of the private soldier.

On the day before the Battle of Königgrätz all the corps commanders were summoned to headquarters; but Von Benedek, after alluding merely to unimportant matters of routine, dismissed them without a word of instruction as to the part to be performed by them in the battle which he must have known to be imminent. On the day of the battle the commanders of the corps and divisions on the right were not informed of the construction of the batteries, and were not notified that these entrenchments were intended to mark their line. Instead of being thrown up by the divisions themselves, these works were constructed by the chief engineer, without one word of consultation or explanation with the corps commanders. Had the commanders of the IIId, IVth and IId Corps been informed that their principal duty would be to guard against a possible, if not probable, advance of the crown prince, it is not likely that the line Cistowes-Maslowed-Horenowes would have been occupied by the right wing; but these generals seem to have taken up their positions with no more idea of their object or of their influence upon the result of the battle than had the men in the ranks.

The selection made by Von Benedek of a field for the coming battle cannot be condemned. On the whole, the position was a strong one, and the fault lay in the dispositions purposely made, or accidentally assumed, rather than in any inherent weakness in the position.

According to some writers, Von Benedek committed an error in holding his advanced posts in the villages on the Bistritz with small forces (which in some cases did not exceed a battalion), while the Prussian advanced-guards generally consisted of a brigade at least. Derrécagaix says:

> It was of importance to the Imperial Army to compel the Prussian forces to deploy at the earliest moment; to tire them before their arrival at the Bistritz; to dispute the passage of that river, which constituted an obstacle, in order that they might approach the main position only after having exhausted their efforts and lost their *élan* through heavy casualties.

To this end, he suggests that the Austrians should have established west of the Bistritz, on the two roads by which the Prussians must necessarily have advanced, two strong advanced posts, composed of troops of all three arms, and sufficiently strong to resist the enemy's advanced-guards. He continues:

> The Bistritz formed a first line of defence, on which it would have been possible to check the assailant's efforts. It possessed the peculiarity of having all along its course villages distant from 1,000 to 1,500 meters, and separated by marshy meadows with difficult approaches. With some batteries in rear of the intervals which separated the villages, it would have been possible to hold them a certain time, and compel the enemy to execute a complete deployment. The Imperial Army had, it is true, on the Bistritz and beyond, detachments of considerable strength. But they played an insignificant part, by reason of the orders given, or modified their positions in the morning. As a result, the line of the Bistritz, its banks, the villages and the woods beyond, were occupied by the Prussians without great efforts, and

they had from that moment defensive *points d'appui* on which it was possible to await events and sustain the fight.

It is impossible to agree fully with Derrécagaix on this point. Speaking of defensible points in front of a position, Hamley says:

A feature of this kind will be especially valuable in front of what would otherwise be a weak part of the position. Strong in itself, and its garrison constantly reinforced from the line; while the ground in front is swept by batteries, such a point is difficult to attack directly; the enemy cannot attempt to surround it without exposing the flank and rear of the attacking troops; and to pass by it in order to reach the position, the assailants must expose their flank to its fire. If several such points exist, they support each other, isolate the parts of the enemy's attack, and force him to expend his strength in costly attacks on them: in fact, they play the part of bastions in a line of fortification. But it is important that they should be within supporting distance and easy of covered access from the rear; failing these conditions, they had better be destroyed, if possible, as defences, and abandoned to the enemy.

Now, none of the advanced posts in question were in front of a weak part of the position (for the line adopted by Von Benedek was incomparably stronger than anything on the line of the Bistritz), and it would have been impossible to use artillery in them with anything like the murderous effect produced by the batteries on the line Lipa-Problus. They were more than a mile and a quarter in front of the position, and were not "easy of covered access from the rear." They were, it is true, within supporting distance of each other; but, while attacking them, the Prussians would have been beyond the best effect of the powerful artillery in the main Austrian line. The preliminary combats would have largely fallen on the infantry; and, owing to the inferior arms and impaired *morale* of his infantry, it was, doubtless, the first aim of the Austrian commander to use his artillery to the fullest extent; for in that arm he knew that he was superior to the Prussians.

Von Benedek's plan was, apparently, to lure Frederick Charles into a position where he should have the Bistritz at his back; where he should be at the mercy of the Austrian artillery; and where he could be overwhelmed by the attack of superior numbers of infantry and cavalry, after he had been demoralized and shattered by a crushing cannonade. The Bistritz (above Lubno) is an insignificant obstacle; but it might have been a troublesome obstruction in the rear of a defeated army. Had the crown prince been delayed five or six hours, it is probable that Von Benedek's plan would have succeeded. The terrible battering which Frederick Charles received, as it actually was, is shown by the fact that his losses exceeded those of the Second Army and the Army of the Elbe combined.

In fact, the event proved that, so far as the repulse of a front attack was concerned, Von Benedek's position fulfilled every condition that could be desired; and it does not seem that anything could have been gained by the occupation in force of the villages on the Bistritz above Lubno. They should rather have been abandoned and destroyed, and everything left to depend on the magnificent position in rear—a position scarcely inferior in strength to Marye's Heights or St. Privat.

The only village on the Bistritz that had any real value was Nechanitz. Von Benedek's weak points were his flanks. Had Nechanitz been occupied in strong force, the turning of the Austrian left by the Army of the Elbe would have been a matter of extreme difficulty, if not a downright impossibility. We have seen that the retreat of the Austrian brigade from Sadowa uncovered the flanks of the advanced posts, and compelled the withdrawal of the troops successively from Dohalitz, Dohalica and Mokrowous; and it might seem, at first, that the abandonment of Nechanitz might have been caused in a similar manner: but such is not the case. The heights in rear of that village, and between it and Hradek, should have been held by two corps, from which a strong detachment should have been placed in Nechanitz. This detachment could easily have been reinforced as occasion demanded.

Any attempt to make a flank attack upon the village, from the direction of Popowitz, would have been made over unfavourable ground, and the attacking force could have been assailed in flank by Austrian troops from the heights. Attempts to cross at Kuncitz or Boharna could have been promptly met and repulsed; and attempts to cross further down would have extended the Prussian front to such a degree as to expose it to a dangerous counter-attack through Nechanitz.

This occupation of Nechanitz would, it is true, have thrust Von Benedek's left flank forward, towards the enemy; but that flank would have been strong in numbers and position; it would have been covered by the Bistritz (where that stream is swollen into a true obstacle); and it would have occupied a position commanding Nechanitz and Kuncitz, and within easy reinforcing distance of each. Nechanitz would have been to Von Benedek's left what Hougomont was to Wellington's right; and in the event of Austrian success, it would have given the same enveloping front that the British had at Waterloo. The neglect of Von Benedek to hold Nechanitz in force is surprising; for the position of his reserves indicates that he expected an attack upon his left—a not unsound calculation, as his main line of retreat lay in rear of his left wing.

On the right there were three positions, any one of which might have been so occupied as to check the attack of the crown prince; namely: 1. The line Trotina-Horenowes; 2. The line Trotina-Sendrasitz-Maslowed; 3. The line Lochenitz-Nedelist-Chlum. The first is regarded as the best by the Austrian Staff. The third is the one actually chosen by Von Benedek, but not taken up, owing to a misunderstanding of orders. Without undertaking to discuss in detail the dispositions that should have been made by the Austrian commander, or the relative merits of the three defensive positions available on the right, the assertion may be ventured that, in order to make them well suited to the ground and the circumstances of the battle, the Austrian dispositions actually made needed only to be modified so as to make the left strong in the vicinity of Nechanitz and the heights of Hradek, and to occupy any one of the three defensive positions on the right with two corps, with another corps in reserve within easy supporting distance.

If then, profiting by American experience, Von Benedek had covered his position with hasty entrenchments (for the construction of which the battle field afforded every facility), he should have been able to repulse the combined Prussian armies; for the numerical odds against him were not great at any time; his reserves would have been in a position to push forward promptly to any point seriously endangered; and his entrenchments would have fully counterbalanced the superior firearms of the Prussian infantry. Though he could not, in all probability, have gained a decisive victory, he could have inflicted greater losses than he received, he could have given his adversaries a bloody check, and the mere possession of a hard-fought field would have raised the *morale* of his depressed army.

For a defensive battle, the formation on a salient angle would, in this case, have been deprived of its usual objections. Considering the nature of the country, and the enormous armies engaged, it is plain that the whole force of the assailant could not be brought to bear on one face of the angle; and the heights of Chlum would have served as a huge traverse to protect the lines from enfilade fire by the enemy's artillery.

A serious defect of the Austrian position was its want of proper extent. As we have seen, the entire army occupied a position only six and three-quarters miles long. Including the reserves, there were, then, more than 30,000 men to a mile. The entire army was crowded, and the cavalry had no room for action. The latter should have operated across the Bistritz against the Prussian right; or (sacrificing itself if necessary) it should have operated against the Prussian left, opposing the advance of the crown prince, and gaining time for the infantry to take up the new position.

The "spectacle of wildest flight and utter rout" in the passage of the defeated army over the Elbe, (as mentioned earlier), would surely seem to support the views of Derrécagaix, rather than those of Hozier, in regard to a position with a river at its back, even though the river be spanned by many bridges. Yet Von Benedek undoubtedly derived considerable advantage from having the Elbe at his back; for the Prussian Staff History says:

> The Elbe formed a considerable barrier to any further immediate pursuit. As soon as the bridges over the river were once reached by the enemy—to whom moreover the fortress of Königgrätz, which commands so large a tract of the surrounding country, afforded a perfectly secure place of crossing—the pursuers were obliged to make the detour by way of Pardubitz.

If Von Benedek had encountered only a front attack, and had been defeated, it is probable that the Elbe at his back would have been advantageous to him in the highest degree; for the superb behaviour of his artillery and cavalry would have effectually covered the retreat of his infantry over the numerous bridges, and the Elbe would have played the same part in favour of the Austrians that the Mincio did after Solferino. But the direction of the crown prince's attack destroyed the value of the bridges north of Königgrätz; and, but for the protection afforded by the fortress, the Elbe, instead of being of the slightest advantage, would have completely barred the retreat of a great part of the Austrian Army.

Von Benedek's selection of his individual station for watching the progress of the battle was unfortunate. From his station on the slope between Lipa and Chlum, his view of the field was limited by the Swiep Wald on the north, and Problus on the south; and his view of the entire northeastern portion of the field was cut off by the hill and village of Chlum. The hill of Chlum was his proper station, and the church tower in that hamlet should have been used as a lookout by some officer of his staff. From that point the Horica Berg, the heights of Horenowes, the Swiep Wald, the village and wood of Sadowa, the villages on the Bistritz (almost as far as Nechanitz), the villages of Langenhof and Problus—in brief, every important part of the field—can be plainly seen. Had this important lookout been utilized, Von Benedek could not have been taken by surprise by the advance of the crown prince. Even the rain, mist and low-hanging smoke could not have wholly obscured the advance of the Second Army from view; for the crown prince was able to trace the direction of the contending lines from the heights of Choteborek, a point much farther from the scene of action than Maslowed and Horenowes are from Chlum. Von Benedek's neglect to make use of the church tower of Chlum probably had not a little to do with the extent of his defeat.

★★★★★★

Although the above comment coincides in its main features with the criticism of Hozier on the same subject, it is based upon the author's own observation of the views of the field afforded from the church tower of Chlum, and from Von Benedek's position near Lipa.

★★★★★★

Among the causes of Prussian success in this campaign, the needle gun has been given a high place by all writers; and Colonel Home, in his admirable *Précis of Modern Tactics*, says:

It is not a little remarkable that rapidity of fire has twice placed Prussia at the head of the military nations of Europe—in 1749 and 1866.

Nevertheless, the importance of the breech-loader in this campaign has probably been over-estimated. The moral and physical effects of the needle gun upon the Austrian soldiers were tremendous, and were felt from the very beginning of the campaign. All other things equal, the needle gun would have given the victory to the Prussians; but all other things were *not* equal. The strategy and tactics of the Prussians were as much superior to those of their opponents as the needle gun was to the Austrian muzzle-loader. In every case, the Prussian victory was due to greater numbers or better tactics, rather than to superior rapidity of fire; and when we consider the tactical features of each engagement, it is hard to see how the result could have been different, even if the Prussians had been no better armed than their adversaries.

The needle gun, undoubtedly, enabled the Prussian Guards to repulse the attacks of the Austrian reserves at Chlum; but the battle had already gone irretrievably against the Austrians, and if they had driven back the Guards, the Ist and Vth Corps would have quickly recovered the lost ground, and the result would have been the same. Derrécagaix, too, overestimates the influence of the needle gun when he points, for proof of its value, to the great disparity of loss between the Prussians and Austrians at Königgrätz. The same enormous disproportion of loss existed in favour of the Germans at Sedan, though the needle gun was notoriously inferior to the Chassepot. This inequality of loss is to be attributed mainly to the superior strategical and tactical movements of the Prussians, by which, in both these battles, they crowded their opponents into a limited space, and crushed them with a concentric fire.

It is a remarkable fact, moreover, that the superiority of the needle gun over the muzzle-loader did not arise so much from the greater rapidity of fire, as from the greater rapidity and security of loading. Baron Stoffel says:

On the 29th of June, 1866, at Königinhof, the Prussians had a sharp action with the enemy. After the action, which took place in fields covered with high corn, Colonel Kessel went over the ground, and to his astonishment, found five or six Austrian bodies for every dead Prussian. The Austrians killed had been mostly hit in the head. His (Kessel's) men, far from firing fast, had hardly fired as many rounds as the enemy. The Austrian officers who were made prisoners said to the Prussians:

'Our men are demoralised, not by the rapidity of your fire, for we could find some means, perhaps, to counterbalance that, but because you are always ready to fire. This morning your men, like ours, were concealed in the corn; but, in this position, yours could, without being seen, load their rifles easily and rapidly: ours, on the other hand, were compelled to stand up and show themselves when they loaded, and you then took the opportunity of firing at them. Thus we had the greatest difficulty in getting our men to stand up at all; and such was their terror when they did stand up to load that their hands trembled, and they could hardly put the cartridge into the barrel. Our men fear the advantage the quick and easy loading of the needle gun gives you; it is this that demoralises them. In action they feel themselves disarmed the greater part of the time, whereas you are always ready to fire.'

As to rapidity of fire, it only remains to add that in the Battle of Königgrätz the number of cartridges fired by the infantry averaged scarcely more than one round per man. This, however, is largely accounted for by the fact that during a great part of the battle the Austrian artillery kept most of Frederick Charles' army beyond effective infantry fire, as well as by the circumstance that a large part of the crown prince's army did not fire a shot—the Vth Corps not coming into action at all.

The needle gun was of inestimable value to the Prussians, but it was by no means the principal cause of their triumph. The great cause of the success of Prussia was, without doubt, the thorough military preparation which enabled her to take the field while her adversaries were yet unprepared, and to begin operations the minute war was declared. This, combined with the able strategy of Von Moltke, enabled the Prussians to seize the initiative; to throw the Austrians everywhere upon the defensive; and to strike them with superior numbers at every move, so that Von Benedek's troops were demoralized before the decisive battle was fought.

The tactics of the Prussians can be best described in the words of Derrécagaix:

In advancing to the attack, the Prussian divisions generally adopted, in this battle, a formation in three groups; the advanced-guard, the centre and the reserve. In the 7th Division, for instance, the advanced-guard consisted of four battalions, four squadrons, one battery and one-half company of pioneers. The centre, or main body, was composed of six battalions and one battery. In the reserve there were one and three-fourths battalions, two batteries and one and one-half companies of pioneers.

These dispositions enabled them to launch against the first points assailed a succession of attacks, which soon gave a great numerical superiority to the assailants. This accounts for the rapidity with which the points of support fell into the hands of the Prussians. Their groups gained the first shelter by defiling behind the rising ground, and when a point was stubbornly defended, the artillery opened fire upon it, while the infantry sought to turn it by pushing forward on the flanks.

On this point Hamley says:

> When it is said that the Prussians are specially alive to the necessity of flank attacks, it is not to be supposed that the turning of the enemy's line alone is meant; for that is a matter for the direction of the commanding general, and concerns only a fraction of the troops engaged. The common application lies in the attack of all occupied ground which is wholly or in part disconnected from the general line, such as advanced posts, hamlets, farm buildings, woods, or parts of a position which project bastion-like, and are weakly defended in flank.

The Prussians seem, in almost every case, to have advanced to the attack in company columns, supported by half-battalion columns, or even by battalions formed in double column on the centre. Though the columns were preceded by skirmishers, the latter seem to have played only the comparatively unimportant part of feeling and developing the enemy; and the present system by which a battle is begun, continued and ended, by a constantly reinforced skirmish line, was not yet dreamed of. It is remarkable that, after witnessing the destructive effects of the needle gun upon their adversaries, the Prussians should have retained their old attack formation, until, four years later, the thickly strewn corpses of the Prussian Guards at St. Privat gave a ghastly warning that the time had come for a change.

It is interesting to compare the tactical features of the campaign of 1866 with those of our own war. The necessity of launching upon the points assailed a succession of attacks was recognized in the tactical disposition frequently made, during the War of Secession, in which the assaulting divisions were drawn up in three lines of brigades, at distances of about 150 yards, the leading brigade being preceded by one, or sometimes two, lines of skirmishers. (For example, the formation of Sedgwick's division at Antietam, Meade's at Fredericksburg, Pickett's at Gettysburg, and Sheridan's at Chattanooga).

The skirmishers being reinforced by, and absorbed in, the first line, the latter, if checked, being reinforced and pushed forward by the second, and the third line being similarly absorbed, the assaulting force, at the moment of collision, generally consisted of all the successive lines merged into one dense line. This formation was the outgrowth of bitter experience in attacking in column, though the attack with battalions ployed in close column had not altogether disappeared in 1864. (See the interesting comments of General J. D. Cox on the assaults in column at Kenesaw Mountain, p. 129, Vol. IX., *Atlanta*, Scribner's *Army and Navy in the Civil War*).

In comparison with the beautiful tactics by which the Germans now attack, with a firing line constantly reinforced from supports and reserves kept in small columns for the double purpose of obtaining the greatest possible combination of mobility and shelter, the attack formation used in the Civil War seems far from perfect; but it was certainly superior to the Prussian attack formation of 1866, for it recognised the hopelessness of attacks in column, and provided for the successive reinforcement of an attacking line. General Sherman, in describing the tactics in use in his campaigns, says:

> The men generally fought in strong skirmish lines, taking advantage of the shape of the ground, and of every cover.

Dispositions being, of course, made for the constant reinforcement of these lines, we find Sherman's army habitually using tactics embracing the essential features of the German tactics of the present day. (See note following).

★★★★★★

The following remarks of Captain F. N. Maude, R. E., on *The Tactics of the American War* sustain the views expressed above, and are interesting as showing an able English military critic's appreciation of the advanced tactical development of the American armies:

> It is curious to note how little attention has been devoted to the study of the fighting of this most bloody of modern wars; and yet it would seem that the records of these campaigns fought out to the bitter end by men of our own Anglo-Saxon races, would be a far more likely source of information, from which to deduce the theory of an attack formation specially designed to meet our needs, than the histories of struggles between French and Germans, or Russians and Turks. Von Moltke is reported to have said that 'nothing was to be learnt from the struggle of two armed mobs.' If that is really the case, which we venture to doubt exceedingly, the great strategist must ere this have been sorry he ever spoke, for, armed mobs or not, both Southern and Northern troops

bore, and bore victoriously, a percentage of loss before which even the best disciplined troops in Germany, the Prussian Guard Corps, failed to make headway. It is of no relevance to the argument to say that the breech-loader was not then in use. When a man is hard hit himself, or sees his comrade rolled over, it never enters his head to consider whether the hit was scored by muzzle-loader or breech-loader; the fact itself, that he or the other man is down, is the only one he concerns himself with, and when the percentage of hits in a given time rises high enough, the attack collapses equally, no matter against what weapon it may be delivered.

Actually, though the armament was inferior, the percentage of hits was frequently far higher than in breech-loading campaigns. There is no action on record during recent years in which the losses rose so high, and in so short a time, as in the American fights.

After a brief description of Meagher's attack at Fredericksburg, and Pickett's charge at Gettysburg, Captain Maude continues:

Surely, Moltke never spoke of such gallant soldiers as an armed mob, seeing that they succeeded in driving an attack home against four times the percentage of loss that stopped the Prussian guard at St. Privat. . . . And assuming, for the moment, that the saying attributed to him is really true, we cannot help fancying that he must have often bitterly regretted it when watching his own men in the manoeuvers of late years, attacking in what is really, practically the same formation which the armed mobs worked out for themselves.

The points of contrast between ourselves and the Americans are far too numerous to be dismissed without comment. They began the war with a drill book and system modelled on our own, and they carried it out to its conclusion, with only a few modifications of detail, but none of principle. The normal prescribed idea of an attack appears to have been as follows: A line of scouts, thickened to skirmishers according to the requirements of the ground; from 200 to 300 paces in rear, the 1st line, two deep, precisely like our own, then in rear a 2nd line and reserve. Of course, their lines did not advance with the steady precision of our old peninsula battalions. Their level of instruction was altogether too low, and besides, the extent of fire-swept ground had greatly increased. Eye witnesses say that after the first few yards, the line practically dissolved itself into a dense line of skirmishers, who threw themselves forward generally at a run as far as their momentum would carry them; sometimes, if the distance was short, carrying the position at the first rush, but more generally the heavy losses brought them to a halt and a standing fire fight ensued. They knew nothing of Scherff's great principle, on which the *Treffen Abstande* or distances between the lines are based, but they generally worked it out in practice pretty successfully. The second line came up in the best order they could and carried the wreck of the first on with them; if they were stopped, the reserve did the same for them, and either broke too, or succeeded.

It will be seen that except in its being more scientifically put together, this German attack is, practically, precisely similar to that employed by the Americans, with the sole difference that the breech-loader has conferred on the assailants the advantage of being able to make a more extended use of their weapons, and has reduced to a certain extent the disadvantage of having to halt.

Had we, in 1871, been thoroughly well informed as to the methods employed across the Atlantic, we should have seen at once that the new weapons did not necessarily entail any alteration in principle in our drill book, and with a little alteration in detail, have attained at one bound to a point of efficiency not reached even in Germany till several years after the war.—*Tactics and Organisation*, by Capt. F. N. Maude, R. E.

★★★★★★

The Austrian infantry tactics possessed the double attribute of antiquity and imbecility. Major Adams, of the Royal Military and Staff Colleges, says:

Since the Italian war, when Napoleon III. declared that 'arms of precision were dangerous only at a distance,' it had been the endeavour of Austria to imitate the tactics to which she attributed her own defeat. If the uniform success of the French in 1859 had established the trustworthiness of the Emperor's theory, how much more necessary must it now be to arrive at close quarters, where precision was accompanied by unusual rapidity of fire? The more recent experiences of the American war would seem indeed to have excited but little interest in Austria. Could it really be reasonably expected that Austrian soldiers should effect what American generals had long discarded as no longer to be attained?

The advocacy of the bayonet, so loudly proclaimed in Austrian circles, would surely have elicited a contemptuous smile from the veterans of the Army of the Potomac. During three years of war, but 143 cases of bayonet wounds were treated in the northern hospitals; of these, but two-thirds were received in action, and six only proved eventually fatal. How, then, could it be imagined that tactics, which had already failed against the common rifle, . . . should now prevail against the Prussian breech-loaders? The manner in which these naked Austrian battalions were ignorantly flung against the murderous fire of the enemy soon produced results which every novice in the art of war will readily appreciate. Even under cover the dread of the Prussian weapon became such that, as the enemy approached, the Austrian infantry either broke or surrendered.

The important aid that the Austrians might have derived from hasty entrenchments has already been pointed out, (as mentioned earlier). In not one single instance did they make use of such shelter-trenches or breastworks as were habitually used by the American armies, though the theatre of war offered the best of opportunities for the quick construction and valuable use of such works. Such attempts at the construction of entrenchments as were made, savour more of the days of Napoleon than of the era of arms of precision. But the Austrians were not alone in their neglect to profit by American experience in this respect. It was not until Osman Pasha showed on European soil the value of hasty entrenchments, that European military men generally took note of a lesson of war that they might have learned thirteen years earlier.

★★★★★★

In Clery's *Minor Tactics* occurs the following astonishing passage:
The use made of entrenchments by the Turks was not
the least remarkable feature of the war of 1877. Field
works, as aids in defence, had been used with advantage
in previous wars, but no similar instance exists of an impregnable system of earthworks being improvised under
the very noses of the enemy.
Col. Clery's book is an evidence of his intelligent study and
thorough knowledge of European military history; yet, as late
as 1885, this professor of tactics at the Royal Military College
at Sandhurst seems not to have heard of Johnston's works at
Kenesaw Mountain, or the fortifications constructed at Spot-
tsylvania and Petersburg

★★★★★★

The great value of hasty entrenchments, and the immeasurable superiority of fire action over "cold steel," were not the only lessons
taught by our war which were unheeded by Austrian soldiers steeped
in conservatism and basking serenely in the sunshine of their own
military traditions. Their use of cavalry showed either an ignorance of,
or contempt for, the experience of the American armies; but, in this
respect, the Austrians were not less perspicacious than their adversaries.
The campaign produced some fine examples of combats between opposing forces of cavalry; but it also produced many instances in which
the Austrians hurled their cavalry against intact infantry armed with
breech-loaders, only to learn from their own defeat and an appalling
list of killed and wounded, that they had applied the tactics of a past age
to the conditions of a new era. Both armies seem to have been afraid
to let their cavalry get out of sight, and to have reserved their mounted
troops solely for use on the field of battle. If they had studied the great
raids of the American cavalry leaders, they would have learned a lesson
which there were excellent opportunities to apply.

It would, probably, have been impossible for the Austrian cavalry
to cut the Prussian communications before the junction of the invading armies was effected. A cavalry column attempting to move around
the left of Frederick Charles would almost certainly have been caught
between the First Army and the impassable Isergebirge, and captured
before doing any damage. A column moving around the Prussian
right, into Saxony, would have encountered the cavalry division of
Von Mülbe's reserve corps, to say nothing of the infantry and artillery;
and the movement would, doubtless, have come to naught.

A movement against the communications of the crown prince could have been made only *via* the valley of the Oder, where it could have been effectually opposed. But it is certain that after the battle of Königgrätz the Austrians had it in their power to balk the advance of Von Moltke by operating with cavalry against his communications. In this case the raiders would have been operating in their own country, and among a friendly population; the railways could have been cut without difficulty, and the cavalry could have retreated without serious danger of being intercepted. The effect upon the invading army does not admit of doubt.

We have seen that, with unobstructed communications, the Prussian Army was subjected to no slight distress, after the battle of Münchengrätz, for want of rations. Even two days after peace had been agreed upon, the Austrian garrison of Theresienstadt, ignorant of the termination of the war, by a successful sally destroyed the railway bridge near Kralup. The line of communication of the Prussians with the secondary base of supplies at Turnau was thus broken; and, though hostilities were at an end, the invaders were subjected to much inconvenience. It is easy to imagine what would have been the effect upon the Prussians during their advance to the Danube, if a Stuart, a Forrest or a Grierson had operated against the railways upon which the supply of the invading army necessarily depended.

Nor were the raiding opportunities altogether on the side of the Austrians. The Prague-Olmütz line of railway, of the most vital importance to Von Benedek, ran parallel to the Silesian frontier, and in close proximity to it. This line of railway should have been a tempting object to a raiding column of cavalry. If it had been cut at any point near Böhmisch-Trübau, the Austrian Army would have been in sore straits for supplies. Vigorous and determined cavalry raids against the railroad between Böhmisch-Trübau and Olmütz would surely have been productive of good results, even if the road had not been cut; for Von Benedek was extremely solicitous about his communications in this part of the theatre (as is shown by his long detention of the IId Corps in this region), and an alert and enterprising raider might have found means of detaining from the main Austrian Army a force much larger than his own.

But neither the Austrian nor the Prussian cavalry was so armed as to be able to make raiding movements with much hope of success. Cavalry without the power of using effective fire-action can never accomplish anything of importance on a raid; for a small force of hostile infantry can easily thwart its objects. The dragoon regiments were armed with the carbine, it is true, but they seem to have been studiously taught to feel a contempt for its use. At Tischnowitz (on the advance from Königgrätz to Brünn) a Prussian advanced-guard, consisting of dragoons, kept off a large force of Austrian cavalry by means of carbine fire, until the arrival of reinforcements enabled the dragoons to charge with the sabre.

According to Hozier, the Austrian cavalry pulled up sharply, "half surprised, half frightened, to find that a carbine could be of any use, except to make noise or smoke, in the hands of a mounted man." Yet nothing seems to have been learned from this incident, and it was not until a brigade of German cavalry, consisting of three regiments, was stopped at the village of Vibray, in December, 1870, by a bare dozen of riflemen, and the *Uhlans* were everywhere forced to retire before the undisciplined *Francs-tireurs*, that the necessity of fire-action on the part of all cavalry was forced home to the Germans. Even yet the strategical value of the American cavalry raids seems to be under-estimated by European military critics, who seem also to regard anything like extensive fire-action on the part of cavalry as scarcely short of military heresy. Von der Goltz says:

> Much has been spoken in modern times of far-reaching excursions of great masses of cavalry in the flank and rear of the enemy, which go beyond the object of intelligence, and have for their aim the destruction of railways, telegraph wires, bridges, magazines and depots. The American War of Secession made us familiar with many such 'raids,' on which the names of a Stuart, an Ashby, a Morgan and others, attained great renown. But, in attempting to transfer them to our theatres of war, we must primarily take into consideration the different nature, civilization and extent of the most European countries, but more especially those of the west.
>
> Then, regard must be paid to the different constitution of the forces. If a squadron of horse, improvised by a partisan, was defeated in such an enterprise, or if, when surrounded by the enemy, it broke itself up, that was of little consequence. It was only necessary that it was first paid for by some successes. Quite a different impression would be caused by the annihilation of one of our cavalry regiments, that by history and tradition is closely bound up with the whole army, and which, when once

destroyed, cannot so easily rise again as can a volunteer association of adventurous farmers' sons.

The thorough organisation of the defensive power of civilized nations is also a preventive to raids. Even when the armies have already marched away, squadrons of horse can, in thickly populated districts, with a little preparation, be successfully repulsed by levies. The French *Francs-tireurs* in the western departments attacked our cavalry, as soon as they saw it isolated.

With all deference to the great military writer here quoted, it is impossible to concede that he has grasped the true idea of cavalry raids. The slight esteem in which he holds "a volunteer association of adventurous farmers' sons" is not surprising, for Europeans have rarely formed a just idea of American volunteers, and the effective fire-action of the American cavalry seems to be taken by foreign critics as proof positive that those troops were not *cavalry*, but merely mounted infantry—a view not shared by those who participated in the sabre charges of Merritt, Custer and Devin. As to the annihilation of a Prussian cavalry regiment, there should be no objection to the annihilation of any regiment, however rich it may be in glorious history and tradition, provided that the emergency demands it, and the results obtained be of sufficient value to justify the sacrifice.

Von Bredow's charge at Mars-la-Tour was deemed well worth the sacrifice of two superb cavalry regiments; yet the results obtained by that famous charge certainly were not greater than those achieved by Van Dorn in the capture of Holly Springs. The former is supposed to have stopped a dangerous French attack; the latter is known to have checked a Federal campaign at its outset. Even had Van Dorn's entire force been captured or slain (instead of escaping without loss) the result would have justified the sacrifice. Nor is the danger of annihilation great, if the cavalry be properly armed and trained. That cavalry untrained in fire-action can be successfully repulsed by levies, in thickly populated districts, is undoubtedly true; but such cavalry as that which, under Wilson, dismounted and carried entrenchments by a charge on foot, would hardly be stopped by such troops as *Francs-tireurs* or any other hasty levies that could be raised in a country covered with villages. Superior mobility should enable cavalry to avoid large forces of infantry, and it should be able to hold its own against any equal force of opposing cavalry or infantry.

The objections of Von der Goltz and Prince Hohenlohe to raids by large bodies of cavalry, lose their force if we consider the cavalry so armed and trained as to be capable of effective fire-action. When cavalry is so armed and organised as to make it possible for Prince Hohenlohe to state that a cavalry division of six regiments "could put only 1,400 carbines into the firing line," and that "in a difficult country it could have no chance against even a battalion of infantry decently well posted," we must acknowledge that a respectable raid is out of the question.

We do not find, in 1866, the cavalry pushed forward as a strategic veil covering the operations of the army. On the contrary we find the cavalry divisions kept well to the rear, and the divisional cavalry alone entrusted with reconnaissance duty, which it performed in anything but an efficient manner. At Trautenau, Von Bonin's cavalry does not seem to have followed the retreat of Mondl, or to have discovered the approach of Von Gablentz. If it was of any use whatever, the fact is not made apparent in history. At Nachod, Steinmetz's cavalry did better, and gave timely warning of the approach of the enemy; but generally, throughout the campaign, the Prussian cavalry did not play a part of much importance either in screening or reconnoitring. It profited greatly by its experience, however, and in the Franco-German war we find it active, alert, ubiquitous, and never repeating the drowsy blunder committed when it allowed Frederick Charles unwittingly to bivouac within four miles and a half of Von Benedek's entire army, or the inertness shown when it permitted the Austrian army to escape from all touch, sight or hearing, for three days, after the Battle of Königgrätz.

On the part of the Austrians, the cavalry was even more negligent and inefficient. Outpost and reconnaissance duties were carelessly performed; and Von Benedek was greatly hampered by a want of timely and correct information of the enemy's movements. In only one instance does the Austrian cavalry seem to have been used profitably; namely, in covering the retreat of the defeated army at Königgrätz. In the words of Hozier:

> Although operations had been conducted in its own country, where every information concerning the Prussian movements could have been readily obtained from the inhabitants, the Austrian cavalry had made no raids against the flank or rear of the advancing army, had cut off no ammunition or provision trains, had broken up no railway communications behind the marching columns, had destroyed no telegraph lines between

the front and the base of supplies, had made no sudden or night attacks against the outposts so as to make the weary infantry stand to their arms and lose their night's rest, and, instead of hovering around the front and flanks to irritate and annoy the pickets, had been rarely seen or fallen in with, except when it had been marched down upon and beaten up by the Prussian advanced-guards.

Surely it needed all the energy and valour shown in the last hours of Königgrätz to atone, in even a small degree, for such inefficiency.

The full offensive value of artillery was not yet understood in any army; and it is not surprising to notice in this campaign the utter absence of the tactics which, in the war with France, brought the German guns almost up to the skirmish line, and kept them actively engaged at close range until the end of the battle. It is, however, amazing to observe the slowness and general inefficiency of the Prussian artillery in every action. At Trautenau, though there were 96 guns belonging to Von Bonin's corps, only 32 were brought into action, while 42 remained in the immediate vicinity without firing a shot. The remaining 22 guns do not seem to have reached the field at all. At Soor the Austrians brought 64 guns into action; but of the 72 guns of the Prussians, only 18 were brought into action from first to last. At Nachod, Skalitz and Gitschin it is the same story—plenty of Prussian artillery, but only a small portion of the guns brought into action, and those without appreciable effect.

Prince Hohenlohe says that in the entire campaign:

The Prussian artillery, which numbered as many pieces as its adversary, had only once been able to obtain the numerical superiority. It had, on all occasions, fought against forces two, three, or even four times superior in number.

At Königgrätz the Prussian artillery was handled with surprising feebleness. The crown prince finally succeeded in bringing to bear on the Austrian right a force of artillery superior in numbers to that opposed to him; but, even in this case, his guns accomplished but little. As to the artillery of Frederick Charles, it practically accomplished nothing at all; and it was scarcely of more use on the Bistritz than it would have been in Berlin. From the beginning to the end of the battle, the Austrians had everywhere a decided superiority of artillery fire, except only in the one case on their right.

The Prussian Staff History says, in regard to the engagement south of the Sadowa wood:

> A want of unity in the direction of the artillery was painfully evident on this part of the field. Two commandants of regiments were on the spot, but the eleven batteries then present belonged to five different artillery divisions, some of them to the divisional artillery and some to the reserve. This accounts for the want of unity of action at this spot; some batteries advanced perfectly isolated, whilst others retired behind the Bistritz at the same time.

To this Colonel Home adds:

> A great deal of this was due to the fact that the guns came into action on one side of a small, muddy, stream, over which there were very few bridges, and across which bridges might have been thrown with ease, while the wagons remained on the other.

It may be further added, that the Prussian artillery seems to have been unduly afraid of encountering infantry fire, and to have had a bad habit of withdrawing to refit and to renew its ammunition. It is said of the Prussian artillery, that "they planted themselves here and there among the reserves, and never found places anywhere to engage." (May's *Tactical Retrospect*).

On the march the artillery was kept too far to the rear, and, owing to its inefficient action, the infantry, long before the close of the campaign, generally showed a disposition to despise its help, and to hurry into action without it, crowding the roads, and refusing to let the guns pass. Much had been expected of their artillery by the Prussians, and its feeble action was a severe disappointment to them. It is to the glory of the Prussians that they were quick to fathom the causes of the inefficiency of their artillery, and that they were able, in four years, to replace the impotence of Königgrätz with the annihilating "circle of fire" of Sedan.

The Austrians far surpassed their adversaries in the skill and effectiveness with which they used their artillery. The superiority of the French artillery had largely contributed to the Austrian disasters in Italy seven years before, and the lesson had not been forgotten. From the beginning of the Campaign of 1866, the Austrian artillery was an important factor in every engagement, and at Königgrätz it was handled superbly. But, in every case, it was used defensively, and the

Austrian artillerists originated no new tactical features, and taught no lessons that could not have been learned from Gettysburg, Malvern Hill, Solferino, or even Wagram.

The concentration of the Prussian armies preparatory to hostilities was made partly by marching, and partly by railroad transportation. The work accomplished by the railroads may, perhaps, be best expressed in the words of the Prussian Staff History:

> The whole of the marches and of the railway movements were so arranged by the General Staff, in harmony with the railway department, that in their execution, in which both the military and civil powers were concerned, no impediments or delays could occur. The result of these arrangements was, that in the twenty-one days allowed, 197,000 men, 55,000 horses, and 5,300 wagons were transported for distances varying between 120 and 300 miles, without any failure, and in such a manner that they attained the required spots at the very hour requisite.

Prussia was thus enabled, in the short space of three weeks, to place 325,000 men on the hostile frontiers, of which number 267,000 were ready for operations against Austria. Yet, great as this achievement was, it shows that the Prussian military system had not yet reached the perfection shown in 1870, when nineteen days sufficed for the mobilisation of an army of 440,000 Germans, and its concentration on the frontier of France.

Further than in the matter of mobilisation and concentration, the use of railways in the Austro-Prussian war presented no new features. In the matter of supplying armies in the field, the small area of the theatre of war, and the inertness of the cavalry, were such that it is almost impossible to make a comparison of the use of railways in this campaign with the use of the same means of transport in the War of Secession. If we imagine a Prussian Army pushing entirely through the Austrian Empire, to the vicinity of Belgrade, and dependent for its supplies on a single line of railway, back to a base on the Prussian frontier; and if we imagine, moreover, that the Austrian cavalry possessed vigilance, enterprise, good firearms and modern ideas, instead of being a mere military anachronism, we can picture a parallel to Sherman's Atlanta campaign.

In regard to the use of the electric telegraph by the Prussians, Hamley says:

> The telegraphic communication between the two Prussian ar-

mies invading Bohemia in 1866 was not maintained up to the Battle of Königgrätz: had it been, and had the situation on both sides been fully appreciated, their joint attack might have been so timed as to obviate the risk of separate defeat which the premature onset of Prince Frederick Charles' army entailed.

Yet Hozier describes in glowing terms the equipment of Frederick Charles' telegraph train, and speaks with somewhat amusing admiration of the feat of placing the Prince's headquarters, at the castle of Grafenstein, in direct telegraphic communication with Berlin, though the castle was five miles from the nearest permanent telegraph station. With each of the Prussian armies was a telegraph train, provided with the wire and other material requisite for the construction of forty miles of line. Yet, though communication was opened between the crown prince and Frederick Charles early on June 30th; though there were three days in which to construct a telegraph line; though the headquarters at Gitschin, Kamenitz and Königinhof could have been put in direct communication without exhausting much more than half the capacity of a single telegraph train, the Prussians neglected even to preserve telegraphic communications to the rear of their armies (and thus with each other *via* Berlin), and, as we have seen, staked their success upon the safe delivery of a message carried by a courier, over an unknown road, on a night of pitchy darkness. Here again a valuable lesson might have been learned from the Americans. (For a description of the American military telegraph, see Grant's *Memoirs*, Vol. II. also the comments on the military telegraph, in Sherman's *Memoirs*, Vol. II.).

Though the War of Secession was begun without military preparation on either side; though its earlier operations sometimes presented features that would have been ludicrous but for the earnestness and valour displayed, and the mournful loss of life which resulted; our armies and generals grew in excellence as the war continued; and before the close of the conflict, the art of war had reached a higher development in America than it attained in Europe in 1866, and, in some respects, higher than it reached in 1870.

Notwithstanding the excellent organisation, the superior arms and thorough preparation of the Prussian armies; notwithstanding the genius of Von Moltke and the intelligence and energy of his subordinates, the prime cause of Austrian failure is found in the neglect of the Austrian generals to watch the development of the art of war on our side of the Atlantic. Had they profited by our experience, their infantry, on one side of the theatre of operations, would have been able, behind entrenchments, to contain many more than their own numbers of the Prussians; and Von Benedek, profiting by his interior lines, could then have thrown superior numbers against the other armies of his adversary. Opposing the Prussian columns with heavy skirmish lines constantly reinforced from the rear, the men of the firing line availing themselves of the cover afforded by the ground, he would have neutralized, by superior tactics, the superior arms of his opponent. His cavalry, instead of using the tactics of a bygone age, would have been used, in part, in cutting the Prussian communications, bringing their advance to a halt, gaining time for him, when time was of priceless value, and enabling him to seize the initiative.

Possibly the war might, nevertheless, have resulted in Prussian success; for Von Moltke has always shown a power to solve quickly, and in the most perfect manner, any problem of war with which he has been confronted, while Von Benedek had only the half-development of a general possessing tactical skill without strategical ability. But the great Prussian strategist would have failed in his first plan of campaign, and he could have been successful only when, like his opponent, he availed himself of the new developments in warfare illustrated by the American campaigns. The Seven Weeks' War would have been at least a matter of months; Austria would not have been struck down at a single blow; other nations might have been drawn into the prolonged conflict, and the entire history of Europe might have been different.

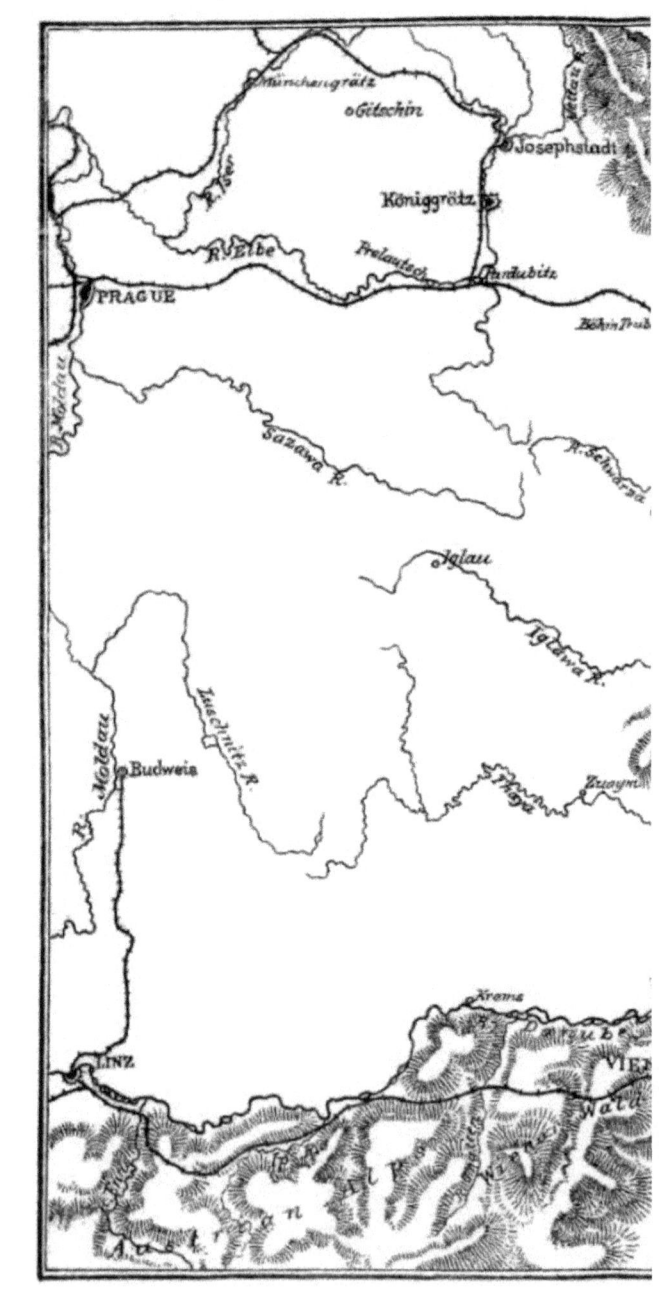

KÖNIGGRÄTZ
TO THE
DANUBE

Glatz

Neisse R.

Olmütz

Prosnitz

Tobitschau

Kremsir

Tischnowitz

Brünn

March R.

Göding

Treutschin

Neustadtl

Nicolsburg

Lundenburg

Lower Carpathians

Wolkersdorf

Wagram

Marchegg

Marchfeld

R. Russbach

Presburg

R. Waag

R. Leitha

Leitha Geb.

Neusiedler
See

Komorn

W. Kilp. Del.

Appendix 1

THE PRUSSIAN ADVANCE FROM KÖNIGGRÄTZ TO THE DANUBE

The day after the Battle of Königgrätz was occupied by the Prussians in resting their fatigued troops, and in separating the mingled corps and detachments of the different armies. Late in the afternoon the first movements in advance began.

The fortresses of Josephstadt and Königgrätz were still in the hands of the Austrians. They were well garrisoned, and could only be taken by siege. Both were summoned to surrender, and both refused. These fortresses were of the greatest importance, as they commanded the line of railway on which the Prussians depended for supplies, and controlled the passage of the Elbe in the vicinity of the battlefield. Strong detachments were, therefore, left to mask the fortresses, and on the 5th of July the Prussian armies marched to Pardubitz and Przelautsch, at which points they crossed the Elbe. A division of *Landwehr* was sent to Prague, which city surrendered, without resistance, on the 8th of July. The Prussians were thus able to open communications with the rear by rail, *via* Pardubitz, Prague, Turnau and Reichenberg, in spite of the fortresses of Theresienstadt, Königgrätz and Josephstadt.

After the Battle of Königgrätz all touch with the Austrians had been lost, and for three days the Prussians were completely in the dark as to the direction taken by the retreating army. On July 6th it was learned that Von Benedek, with the greater portion of his army, had retreated upon Olmütz.

After the battle two lines of retreat were open to Von Benedek. It was desirable to retreat upon Vienna, for the double purpose of protecting the city, and effecting a junction with the victorious troops, withdrawn from Italy for the defence of the capital. (A brief sketch of the operations in Italy is given in Appendix 3). But Vienna was 135 miles distant; the army had been heavily defeated; and there was danger that a retreat of such a distance would degenerate into a demoralised rout. Olmütz was only half as far away; its fortress would afford the necessary protection for reorganising and resting the army; and its position on the flank of the Prussians would be a serious menace to their communications, in case of their advance on Vienna. Von Benedek, therefore, retreated upon Olmütz, sending the Xth Corps by rail to Vienna, and the greater part of his cavalry by ordinary roads to the same point.

The situation was now favourable to Von Moltke. He had the advantage of interior lines, and he did not hesitate to make use of them. Yet the problem was by no means devoid of difficulties. The Austrian army at Olmütz was still formidable in numbers; the extent of its demoralization was not known; the Austrian troops had a high reputation for efficiency, and for a capacity to present an undaunted front after a defeat; and it was thought possible that Von Benedek might assume the offensive.

To leave such a formidable army unopposed on his flank was not to be thought of; yet it was desirable to reach Vienna before the arrival at that city of the troops recalled from Italy, or, at any rate, before a considerable army could be concentrated for the defence of the capital. A division of the Prussian forces was, therefore, necessary. The Army of the Elbe and the First Army were directed upon Vienna: the former to move *via* Iglau and Znaym; the latter, *via* Brünn. The crown prince was directed upon Olmütz to watch Von Benedek. There were three courses open to the Austrian commander:

1. To attack the flank of the First Army, between Olmütz and Vienna; 2. To withdraw rapidly to the capital; 3. To attack the crown prince.

In the first case, the First Army would be supported by the Army of the Elbe, and the combined forces would be able to take care of themselves. In the second case, the crown prince was to attack the retiring army and harass its march. In the third case, the crown prince, who, though inferior in numbers, was superior in *morale*, might be more than a match for the Austrians. In case of defeat, however, he was to retreat into Silesia, where he would have the support of the Prussian fortresses; while Von Moltke, freed from Von Benedek, could seize the Austrian capital and command peace.

On July 7th the cavalry of the Second Army recovered touch with the Austrians, and there was some skirmishing with their rear guards.

On July 8th the Austrian Government made overtures for an armistice of not less than eight weeks, nor more than three months; as a condition to which the fortresses of Königgrätz and Josephstadt were to be surrendered. The proposition was rejected by the Prussians, who continued to advance.

Von Benedek was relieved from the chief command of the Austrian army, being superseded by Archduke Albrecht, who had won the victory of Custozza over the Italians. Von Benedek retained command, however, until the arrival of his army on the Danube. The Austrians were now straining every nerve to assemble an army at Vienna. Leaving only one corps and one division in Italy, the Archduke's army had been recalled from Venetia, and was proceeding, by rail and by forced marches, to the Danube.

On the 11th of July Von Benedek's army was ordered to Vienna. This army, after a continuous retreat of eight days' duration, had just completed its concentration at Olmütz; but the movement to Vienna was begun without delay, the IIId Corps being sent on the day the order was received. The withdrawal of the army from Olmütz to Vienna was not an easy operation. The railway was, as yet, beyond the reach of the Prussians; but the aid that it could lend was not great. It was estimated that the withdrawal of the entire army by the single line of railway would require a full month. Part of the troops were, accordingly, hurried on by rail, and the bulk of the army was ordered to march by the valley of the March to Pressburg.

This was the most direct route, and the one which offered the best roads for marching, though by taking this line the Austrian army would expose a flank to the attack of the Prussians. Above all things, celerity was necessary, in order that the march might be completed without fatal interruption. Von Benedek's army marched in three echelons. The first, composed of the IId and IVth Corps, with the greater part of the Saxon cavalry, started on the 14th of July. The second, consisting of the VIIIth and Ist Corps, left the next day; and the third, made up of the VIth Corps and the Saxons, followed on the 16th.

The Austrian cavalry presented a bold front to the Prussian armies moving on Vienna, and a sharp action was fought at Tischnowitz, on the 11th of July, between the cavalry of Frederick Charles' advanced-guard and a division of Austrian lancers, resulting in the defeat of the latter. On the 12th Frederick Charles took possession of Brünn without resistance. The next day, after some skirmishing with the Austrian cavalry, the Army of the Elbe occupied Znaym.

After a rest of two days, the Army of the Elbe and the First Army continued their march towards the Danube; the former being directed towards Krems, the latter moving *via* Nikolsburg.

The Austrian troops from Italy began to arrive at Vienna on the 14th of July. In the meantime, the crown prince, hearing of Von Benedek's withdrawal from Olmütz, directed his march on Prerau, and, on the 14th, reached Prosnitz, about twelve miles south of Olmütz. The first Austrian echelon, marching by the right bank of the March, just escaped serious collision with the crown prince, the cavalry of the Second Army skirmishing with the Saxon cavalry, and becoming engaged with a battalion of infantry on the flank of the Austrian IId Corps.

On the following day Von Bonin, with the Ist Corps and Von Hartmann's cavalry division, attacked the second echelon of Von Benedek's army, and defeated it in the actions of Tobitschau and Rokienitz. As a result of these actions, the right bank of the March was no longer available for the Austrian retreat. Von Benedek had, however, succeeded in slipping away from the crown prince, though at the expense of losing his best and most direct road to Vienna.

Learning that large bodies of Austrians had been seen moving south from Olmütz for some days, Von Moltke saw at once that it would be impossible to bar Von Benedek's path with the Second Army, and immediately ordered the First Army to Lundenburg. The railway and telegraph at Göding were cut by a detachment of Prussian cavalry, on the 15th, and Frederick Charles occupied Lundenburg the next day.

This was a severe blow to Von Benedek, for he thus lost his railway communication with Vienna, his march by the valley of the March was headed by the Prussians, and he was compelled to make a detour by crossing the Carpathian Mountains and following the valley of the Waag. To compensate, as far as possible, for the loss of the shorter road, Von Benedek hastened his troops by forced marches. Von Moltke did not deem it prudent to send the Second Army after Von Benedek into the valley of the Waag, as communication between the crown prince and Frederick Charles would thus be lost, and it was now desirable to concentrate rather than separate. It was accordingly determined to push forward with all available troops to the Danube.

The crown prince had already seen the impossibility of thwarting Von Benedek's retreat, and, as early as the 15th, had left the Ist Corps to mask Olmütz, had directed the Vth Corps and a cavalry division to follow on the flank of Von Benedek, and had pushed forward with the rest of his army upon Brünn, where he arrived on the 17th. On the same day the Army of the Elbe and the First Army were in the neighbourhood of Nikolsburg.

On the 19th the heads of the Prussian Armies were within less than two days' march of the Austrian capital, but part of the Prussian forces were as far back as Brünn. Von Moltke did not know, to a certainty, how much of Von Benedek's army had been brought back from Olmütz before the obstruction of the railway. A large part of it might already be in his front; he knew that large bodies of troops had come in from Italy; the fortifications of Florisdorf were extensive; and it seemed possible that the Austrians might, by a last great effort, have assembled an army large enough to enable them to push forward from Florisdorf, to deliver battle on the Marchfeld for the defense of their capital. With the double object of preparing to attack and being in readiness to receive an attack, Von Moltke ordered the Army of the Elbe to Wolkersdorf, the First Army to Wagram, and the Second Army in reserve at Schönkirchen.

The Prussian Army was thus concentrated behind the Russbach, in position to meet an attack of 150,000 Austrians from Florisdorf; to reconnoitre and attack the Florisdorf entrenchments; or to leave a corps of observation in front of them and push to the left and seize Pressburg. The Second Army, with the exception of the Vth Corps, was to be in position to support the other two by the 21st. The Vth Corps was to be hurried up as rapidly as possible, in order that the entire army might be concentrated for a decisive battle.

The only troops of Von Benedek's army which had reached Vienna by the 20th were the Xth and IIId Corps, part of the Saxons, and four cavalry divisions, numbering altogether from 55,000 to 60,000 men. The reinforcements from Italy which had arrived at the capital numbered about 50,000 men.

Although the occupation of Pressburg was absolutely necessary to secure the prompt junction of the divided Austrian armies, that important point was held by only a single brigade. As soon as the Austrian IId Corps had reached Tyrnau, its leading brigade was pushed forward rapidly, in country carts, to reinforce the brigade at Pressburg, and the rest of the corps hastened towards the same place by forced marches. If Pressburg fell into the hands of the Prussians, the force still with Von Benedek, constituting the bulk of his army, would not be able to reach Vienna, and form a junction with the Archduke Albrecht, except by making a long detour *via* Komorn, and would probably be delayed so long as to be helpless to prevent the capture of the capital.

On the 21st of July the Army of the Elbe and the First Army were in position behind the Russbach, and the Second Army was drawing near, its two advanced corps being not more than one day's march distant. The situation of the Austrians was critical. Their IId Corps had not yet reached Pressburg, and that all-important point was still held by only two brigades. The Ist, VIth and VIIIth Corps, and a division of Saxons, had gotten no farther than Neustadtl and Trentschin, nearly sixty miles from Pressburg. On the same day Von Fransecky, with the Prussian IVth Corps and a cavalry division, crossed the March, in the vicinity of Marchegg, advancing upon Pressburg. Everything portended to the Austrians the loss of that valuable strategic point, and the consequent cutting off of Von Benedek from Vienna.

The Prussian Army, numbering, at least, 184,000 men, was concentrated and opposed to an army of not more than 110,000 men, at most, at Vienna. The capture of the capital seemed certain; and Von Moltke, with his forces augmented to 200,000 men, by the reinforcements that were pushing on to join him, could then turn upon Von Benedek, and give a *coup de grace* to the last remnant of Austria's military power.

At this junction, however, diplomacy stepped in, and, through the mediation of France, a five days' armistice, as a preliminary to peace, was agreed upon; the armistice to go into effect at noon on the 22nd of July.

On the 22nd Von Fransecky struck the two Austrian brigades at Blumenau, just in front of Pressburg. While everything was going in favour of the Prussians, and they seemed to be not only on the point of defeating the Austrians, but of capturing their entire force, the hour of noon arrived; the armistice went into effect, the action was, with difficulty, broken off, and, after the sudden termination of the battle, both armies bivouacked on the field.

The preliminary terms of peace were signed at Nikolsburg on the 26th of July, and definitely ratified at Prague on the 30th of August. The orders for the withdrawal of the Prussian armies were issued on the 25th of August, and the Austrian territory was entirely evacuated by them by the 20th of September.

By the terms of the treaty of peace, Venetia was ceded to Italy; the old Germanic confederation was dissolved; Schleswig-Holstein became the property of Prussia; Austria consented to the formation of a North German Confederation, and a union of the South German States, from both of which confederations she was to be excluded; and the defeated power agreed to pay 40,000,000 Prussian *thalers* to the

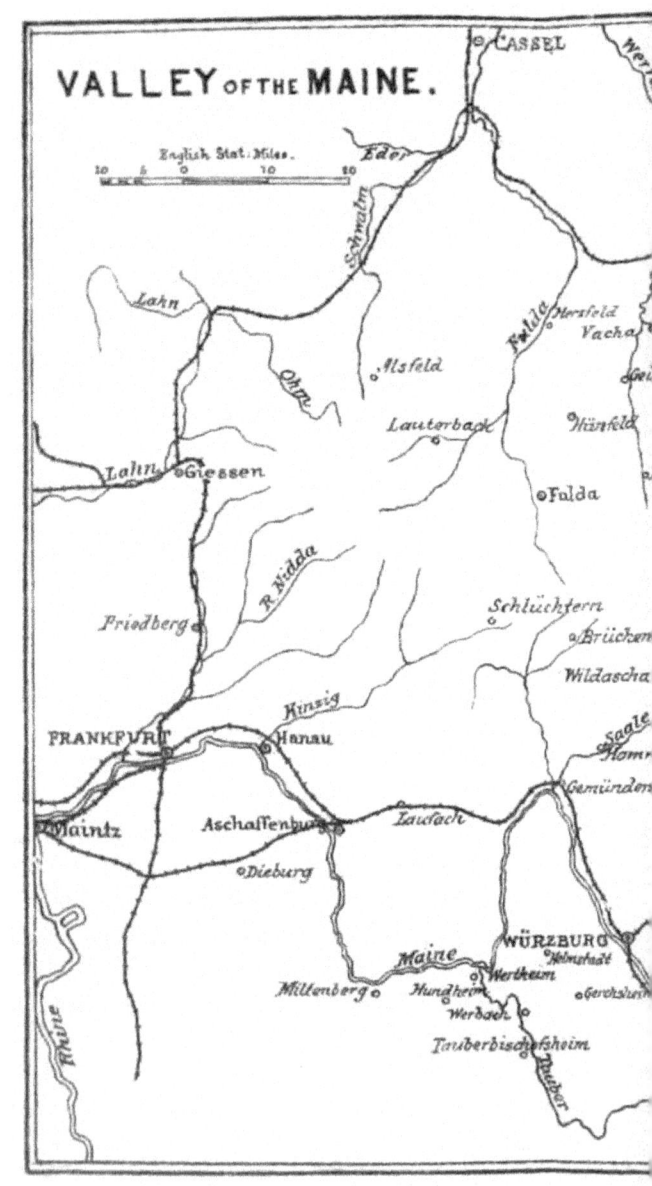

Unstrut

Langensalza

Eisenach   GOTHA   WEIMAR

oDermbach
Mosenthal

sa

RUDOLSTADT

Saale

Hilders

MEININGEN

oSchleusingen

Hildburghausen

au

Neustadt

Kissingen

COBURG

Rodach

elburg

R. Main

Schweinfurt

Main

Baireuth

Bamberg

Regnitz

N

W   E

S

Nürnberg

W. Kilp, Del.

victor. From this sum, however, 15,000,000 *thalers* were deducted as the price of the Austrian claims to Schleswig-Holstein, and 5,000,000 *thalers* for the free maintenance of the Prussian Army in the Austrian provinces from the preliminary truce to the final establishment of peace. Peace with the German allies of Austria was made at about the same time. As a result of the war, Prussia annexed the territories of Hanover, Hesse-Cassel, Nassau and the free city of Frankfort. The population of the victorious kingdom was increased by 4,285,700 people; and its area, by nearly 25,000 square miles of land.

Appendix 2

THE CAMPAIGN IN WESTERN GERMANY

The surrender of the Hanoverian Army at Langensalza, on June 29, 1866, left Von Falckenstein free to operate against the armies of the South German States. His army, now designated "The Army of the Maine," numbered 45,000 men and 97 guns.

Opposed to him were the Bavarian Corps, numbering 40,000 men and 136 guns, and the VIIIth Federal Corps, numbering 46,000 men and 134 guns. The former, under the command of Prince Charles of Bavaria, had concentrated at Schweinfurt; the latter, under the command of Prince Alexander of Hesse, at Frankfort.

Having been informed that the Hanoverians were marching on Fulda, Prince Charles began a forward movement, to effect a junction with them at that point; but receiving later news to the effect that the occupation of Hesse-Cassel had caused the Hanoverians to turn off towards Mühlhausen, and that Prussian forces were concentrating at Eisenach, he decided to direct his march more to the right, so as to be able to operate either by way of Fulda or the Thuringian Forest (*Thüringer Wald*), as circumstances might decide. The march of the Bavarians was begun on June 22nd; but much was wanting to complete their organisation and equipment, and their progress was so slow that on the 26th their most advanced division had only reached Neustadt, on the Saale, scarcely twenty miles from Schweinfurt.

A prompt union of the separated forces of the allies was of the utmost importance. Yet the most precious time was aimlessly wasted, and it was not until June 26th that any definite steps were taken towards effecting a junction of the Bavarians and the VIIIth Corps. On that day Prince Charles and Prince Alexander held a conference, at which it was decided to move forward and effect the junction of the two corps at Hersfeld, about twenty-one miles north of Fulda. They overlooked the important fact that they were twice as far away from the designated point as the Prussians were.

Nothing but the most energetic action on the part of the allies could overcome the disadvantages of their strategical situation. Yet Prince Charles, learning that negotiations were being conducted between the Hanoverians and the Prussians, delayed his march, evidently losing confidence in the sincerity of his allies, and fearing that a surrender of the Hanoverians might leave him to contend alone with Von Falckenstein. For three days the Bavarians remained inactive; then, hearing of the Battle of Langensalza, Prince Charles advanced towards Gotha. On June 30th the Bavarians had advanced to Meiningen, Schleusingen and Hildburghausen, where they received news of the surrender of the Hanoverian Army. The VIIIth Corps, in the meantime, had continued its march towards Hersfeld.

The march of Prince Charles towards Gotha had been utterly fruitless. He had not only failed to assist the Hanoverians, but time had been lost, and the direction of his march had carried him away from, instead of towards, the VIIIth Corps. The latter corps was now at Friedburg, more than 80 miles from Meiningen, and the problem of effecting a junction now presented many difficulties. The union of the two corps could have been easily and safely effected by falling back to the line of the Maine; and this should have been done, though it was feared that a retreat, at the beginning of the campaign, and before the enemy had been seen, might have an injurious effect on the *morale* of the troops. To effect a junction without falling back would necessitate a flank march of more than 80 miles, over difficult mountain roads, in the immediate front of the enemy. Such a hazardous movement should not have been undertaken except as a last resort.

Nevertheless, Prince Charles decided to form line at Meiningen, facing Eisenach, hoping to join the VIIIth Corps *via* Hilders-Fulda and Geisa-Hünfeld, and requesting Prince Alexander to draw towards him with all available forces, partly *via* Hanau-Fulda-Hünfeld, and partly by rail from Frankfort to Gemünden, and thence *via* Hammelburg to Kissingen. The commander of the VIIIth Corps consented to move on Fulda, but did not see fit to send a force *via* Kissingen to the neighbourhood of Schweinfurt, evidently for the military reason that he did not wish to divide his force while executing a dangerous movement, and for the political reason that the movement urged by Prince Charles, while it would cover Bavaria, would expose the territories of the contingents which composed the VIIIth Corps. Prince Charles showed a disposition to ignore the interests of his allies; Prince Alexander exhibited decided insubordination; both commanders displayed a lack of military ability; and the want of hearty co-operation between the two generals already portended disaster to the allied cause.

On July 1st the Bavarians concentrated at Meiningen, and began their march to Fulda. Prince Alexander, marching east, occupied Lauterbach and Alsfeld on July 3rd. His force had been diminished by detachments left on the Lahn, both to cover Frankfort from a possible attack from the direction of Cassel, and to protect the flank and rear of the army marching towards Fulda.

On July 3rd a Bavarian advanced-guard found Dermbach in possession of the Prussians, and was driven back with some loss. On the other hand, a Prussian detachment was driven out of Wiesenthal. Von Falckenstein had advanced from Eisenach on July 1st, and he was now in the immediate front of the Bavarians; Von Beyer's division in and around Geisa; Von Goeben's division at Dermbach, and Von Manteuffel's division following in reserve.

On July 4th one of Von Goeben's brigades struck a Bavarian division at Zella (about 3 miles south of Dermbach), and an indecisive action followed. With his other brigade, Von Goeben attacked another Bavarian division at Wiesenthal. Encountering considerable resistance, and having no immediate supports at hand, Von Goeben gave orders for the withdrawal of his troops, after an action of some hours' duration. At the same time the Bavarians retreated, and the field was abandoned by both armies.

During this time the other Prussian divisions continued their march on Fulda, Von Beyer reaching Hünfeld, near which place his advanced-guard had a remarkable combat with the Bavarian reserve cavalry, which had been sent from Schweinfurt towards Vacha, to open communications with the VIIIth Corps. The Bavarian advanced-guard consisted of two regiments of *cuirassiers* and a detachment of horse artillery. On meeting the Prussians, the Bavarians opened on them with grape. The artillery with Von Beyer's advanced-guard quickly came into action, and opened fire with astonishing results; for the first shot from the Prussian guns sent the Bavarians back in a wild panic, the confusion being rapidly conveyed from the advanced-guard to the main body, until the entire force (consisting of three brigades) broke into a headlong stampede. Several regiments retreated as far as Brückenau and Hammelburg, and many troopers did not draw rein until they arrived at the Maine, many miles from the scene of action.

Several days elapsed before the cavalry could be rallied at Brückenau. In this case the Bavarians could neither plead surprise nor heavy loss. They saw their enemy in time to open fire on him first; and their total loss was only 28 men. Only a few shots, from two guns, were fired by the Prussians before the Bavarian cavalry had scampered beyond reach of harm.

The simultaneous retreat of both armies from Wiesenthal reminds one of the *fiasco* at Big Bethel in 1861; and had the Bavarians remained on the field at Hünfeld long enough to dot the ground thickly with dead and wounded, their action there might be worthy of comparison with that of our undisciplined levies at Bull Run.

After the combat at Wiesenthal, Von Falckenstein seems to have felt considerable anxiety; for the next day he withdrew Von Goeben through Dermbach, recalled Von Beyer to Geisa, and brought up Von Manteuffel in close support. This concentration was evidently made with a view to fighting a defensive battle; but, on the 6th of July, the Prussians discovered that they had won a victory on the 4th, the Bavarians being in retreat. Von Falckenstein at once pushed forward towards Fulda.

After the actions of Zella and Wiesenthal Prince Charles saw that the intended junction of the separated corps at Fulda could not be made, unless he could open the road by defeating the Prussians. This now seemed out of the question; and he, consequently, fell back on Neustadt, and requested Prince Alexander to open communications with him *via* Brückenau and Kissingen. Prince Alexander, however, does not seem to have been over-anxious either to comply with requests or to obey orders. On July 5th he had advanced to within seven miles of Fulda. Hearing of the Bavarian reverses, he fell back to Schlüchtern, where he occupied an exceptionally favourable position at the entrance of the Kinzig valley. The ground offered every facility for defense; he could offer a stubborn resistance to the advance of Von Falckenstein; his line of retreat to Frankfort was secure; and he might either wait for the Bavarians to join him, or effect a junction with them on the line Hammelburg-Gemünden.

While at Schlüchtern, Prince Alexander learned of the Austrian defeat at Königgrätz; and, without considering his allies, his only thought seems to have been to gain the line of the Maine, between Hanau and Mayence, where he might protect the territories of Southwest Germany. How far he was influenced by his own judgment, and how far by the Diet at Frankfort, is not known; but he abandoned his strong position at Schlüchtern, and fell back to Frankfort, where he was joined by the detachments which had been left on the Lahn. Instead of concentrating to oppose the Prussians, the allies thus voluntarily widened the gap between their forces, and wilfully invited destruction.

The Prussians entered Fulda on the 7th of July, and rested there one day. From Fulda, Von Falckenstein directed Von Goeben on Brückenau, and sent Von Beyer out on the Frankfort road to Schlüchtern, Von Manteuffel occupying Fulda. The movement to Schlüchtern was for the double purpose of making a feint towards Frankfort, and gaining a separate road for the advance of the division. From Schlüchtern Von Beyer marched direct to the suburbs of Brückenau. Von Goeben marched through and beyond Brückenau, and Von Manteuffel, following, occupied the town. The Army of the Maine was now closely concentrated within nine miles of the Bavarians, who were extended along the Saale, from Neustadt to Hammelburg, occupying a line 22½ miles long.

On July 10th Von Falckenstein directed Von Beyer on Hammelburg and Von Goeben on Kissingen. Von Manteuffel was ordered to move on Waldaschach, and then to follow Von Goeben. The Bavarians were encountered at Hammelburg and Kissingen, and defeated with some loss. Minor actions, with similar results, were fought on the same day at Friedrichshall, Hausen and Waldaschach, up the river from Kissingen. The Bavarians retreated to Schweinfurt and Würzburg, and the passes of the Saale remained in the hands of the Prussians.

All military principles now dictated an advance against Schweinfurt, for the purpose of giving the Bavarians a crushing defeat, and disposing of them altogether. Such a move would, doubtless, have been made by Von Falckenstein, had not political considerations been at this time paramount. The Prussian victories in Austria rendered it probable that peace conferences would soon be held; and, at the request of Bismarck, Von Falckenstein was notified that it was of political importance to be in actual possession of the country north of the Maine, as negotiations would probably soon take place on the *statu quo* basis. Von Falckenstein, therefore, decided to move against the VIIIth Corps, for the purpose of clearing the right bank of the Maine entirely of the hostile forces.

Prince Alexander, thoroughly alarmed at the condition of affairs, now sought to form a junction with the Bavarians at Würzburg, *via* Aschaffenburg and Gemünden. As a preliminary to this movement, a

Hessian brigade was sent to Aschaffenburg, to secure the passage of the Maine at that point, and to reconnoitre the Prussians. The contemplated movement was hopeless from the start, unless the Bavarians could render assistance by advancing to Gemünden; and, after the actions on the Saale, they were not in a condition to do so. As it was, Prince Alexander was endeavouring to cross the difficult mountain region between Aschaffenburg and Gemünden, in the face of a victorious army, superior to his own in numbers and *morale*, to effect a junction with an ally who was unable to lend him a helping hand. It was the height of folly; for the junction could have been easily and safely made south of the Maine. True, this would have necessitated the sacrifice of Frankfort; but defeat north of the Maine would compel the evacuation of the city, and defeat was now practically invited.

Turning away from the Bavarians, Von Falckenstein moved down the Maine; Von Goeben in advance, followed by Von Manteuffel, while Von Beyer moved, by way of the Kinzig valley, on Hanau. On July 13th the Hessian brigade was defeated by Von Goeben at Laufach, and fell back on Aschaffenburg, to which place reinforcements were hurried by Prince Alexander. On the following day the VIIIth Corps was defeated by Von Goeben at Aschaffenburg. The brunt of the battle was borne by an Austrian brigade attached to the Federal Corps; but few troops of the Hessian contingents being engaged, and the Würtemberg and Baden troops arriving too late. Had Prince Alexander concentrated his entire force at Aschaffenburg, the result might have been bad for the Prussians, for their march was so unskilfully conducted that Von Goeben was without support; the other detachments of Von Falckenstein's army being more than thirty miles in rear. The Prussians did not pursue the enemy, but contented themselves with remaining in possession of the field.

Prince Alexander was now convinced of the impossibility of effecting a junction at Würzburg *via* Aschaffenburg. He accordingly abandoned the line of the Lower Maine and concentrated his force at Dieburg. Frankfort was thus left defenceless, and the remnants of the German Diet fled to Augsburg. Prince Charles now proposed a junction of the allies in the vicinity of Würzburg, the VIIIth Corps to move *via* Miltenberg and Tauberbischofsheim, and the concentration to be effected on the 20th of July. This movement necessitated a march of some ninety miles for the VIIIth Corps, and the uncovering of Southwest Germany, while the Bavarians had to march only a few miles, and continued to cover their own territories; but the imminent danger which now threatened the VIIIth Corps caused Prince Alexander to forget local and personal jealousies, and strive to effect the junction which the military situation imperatively demanded.

On the 16th of July the Prussians entered Frankfort, where they remained until the 21st: Von Goeben's division occupying the city, Von Beyer's division being stationed at Hanau, and Von Manteuffel's division holding Aschaffenburg. The entire region north of the Maine was in the possession of the Prussians. Frankfort had been especially antagonistic to Prussia, and it now felt the full force of the severity of the conquerors. Von Falckenstein levied a contribution of $3,000,000 on the city, and soon followed this heavy exaction by a demand for a second enormous contribution of $10,000,000. The King of Prussia, however, remitted the second contribution after hearing the appeal and protest of the citizens.

On the 16th of July Von Falckenstein was relieved from the command of the Army of the Maine, and appointed military governor of Bohemia. He was succeeded by Von Manteuffel, whose division was placed under command of Von Flies. Reinforcements now raised the Army of the Maine to a strength of 50,000 men and 121 guns.

The capture of Frankfort and the possession of the country north of the Maine had been obtained at the sacrifice of the great strategic advantage enjoyed by the Prussians. It was no longer possible to prevent the concentration of the VIIIth Corps and the Bavarians, and on the 22nd of July this junction was completed; the former corps holding the line of the Tauber, and the latter occupying a position between that river and Würzburg.

Although the allied forces now numbered 80,000 men and 286 guns, Von Manteuffel decided to move against them from Frankfort. The advantage of the allies was in numbers alone; in *morale*, and in the strategic situation, the advantage was with the Prussians. Von Manteuffel now had a line of communication through Frankfort and Cassel. Though he could no longer keep the allies asunder, he could, by marching to the Tauber, compel them to "form front to a flank," while his own front securely covered his communications. His communications could be intercepted only by a movement of the allies north of the Maine, which would reciprocally expose their own.

The allies had hardly effected their junction, when a want of harmony in the views of their commanders again became evident. An offensive movement against the Prussians was agreed upon; but Prince Charles wished to move by the left bank of the Maine on Frankfort, while Prince Alexander preferred a movement by the right bank on Aschaffenburg. The former was, doubtless, the better move—at all events it was the safer; for the allies would have covered their communications better, and a junction might, perhaps, have been effected with the large garrison of Mayence—but, after two days of discussion and deliberation, the latter movement was agreed upon. In the meantime, while the allies were deliberating, Von Manteuffel was acting; and he was now moving rapidly towards the Tauber.

On July 23rd the Prussians touched the enemy. A slight and indecisive action was fought by a Prussian advanced-guard with the Baden division at Hundheim, and the advanced troops of the VIIIth Corps were pressed back along their whole line. While the Prussians were thus closing upon the Federal Corps, the Bavarians began the contemplated movement by the right bank of the Maine; one division being sent by rail to Gemünden, another to Lohr (on the right bank, farther down), and part of a third to Wertheim. Thus the junction of the allies, which had been effected with such difficulty, was voluntarily broken at the very moment of contact with the enemy. The line of the allied forces, on the evening of July 23rd, was 36 miles in extent; while Von Manteuffel's army was closely concentrated in their immediate front. Prince Alexander, finding himself beyond the immediate assistance of the Bavarians, withdrew all his detachments behind the Tauber, where his corps was spread over a space seven miles in breadth and nine in depth, in a country full of deep ravines, which rendered prompt movements, especially of cavalry and artillery, quite out of the question.

On the 24th Von Goeben defeated the Würtembergers at Tauberbischofsheim, and the Baden division at Werbach. The retreat of the Baden troops uncovered Prince Alexander's right flank, and there was now imminent danger of the Prussians again pushing in and separating the VIIIth Corps from the Bavarians. Prince Alexander, therefore, fell back to Gerchsheim, and the Bavarians withdrew to Helmstadt. Prince Charles ordered the VIIIth Corps back to the line of the Tauber, though the Bavarians could render no immediate assistance. Prince Alexander, doubtless appreciating the folly of attempting, without reinforcements, to dislodge the victorious Prussians from a position which he had been unable to hold against them, seems to have paid no attention to the order, for he proceeded at once to concentrate his scattered divisions at Gerchsheim.

On July 25th Von Goeben formed the right of the Prussian line,

Von Beyer the centre and Von Flies the left. Von Goeben was to attack the VIIIth Corps in front, while Von Beyer turned its right and cut it off from Würzburg. Von Flies was to keep his division concentrated on the left; for nothing was known of the whereabouts of the Bavarians, and it was surmised that they might be somewhere in that direction.

Von Beyer, moving against the VIIIth Corps, unexpectedly encountered a Bavarian division at Helmstadt, and defeated it, after an engagement which lasted some hours. While the Prussians were resting on the field, after the action, a second Bavarian division suddenly appeared on the crest of a hill in the rear of Von Beyer's left wing. So completely was Von Beyer without information as to the position of the Bavarians, that he was in doubt whether these troops were friend or foe. The Bavarians were in a similar quandary. In fact, they had accidentally stumbled upon the Prussians, and the surprise was mutual. As soon as he discovered that he was in the presence of a hostile force, Von Beyer executed a change of front to the left, and succeeded in gaining another victory.

While Von Beyer was engaged with the Bavarians, Von Goeben was battling with the VIIIth Corps at Gerchsheim. Prince Alexander was again defeated, and driven in rout on Würzburg.

The night after these actions Prince Charles held a council of war, and finally decided to attack Von Flies, who, having advanced, was now on the Prussian left. Learning, however, that his own left had been uncovered by the defeat of the VIIIth Corps, the Bavarian commander resolved to stand on the defensive on the plateau of Waldbüttelbrünn (in rear of Rossbrünn, a place not marked on the map but about 7 miles due west of Würzburg.), and ordered Prince Alexander to take up a position immediately in front of Würzburg, to cover the retreat of the army across the Maine, should such a movement be necessary.

About 3 o'clock on the morning of July 26th, a simultaneous attempt of the Bavarians and Von Flies to occupy some commanding ground which lay between the outposts, brought on an action at Rossbrünn. While Von Flies was engaged with the Bavarians, Von Beyer struck them heavily on the flank, and by 10 o'clock the Bavarians were in full retreat. The Prussians did not attempt a pursuit, and by 1 o'clock, p.m., Prince Charles had rallied and concentrated his corps on the plateau of Waldbüttelbrünn. In the meantime, the VIIIth Corps had crossed the Maine.

The position of the Bavarians was now full of peril. Their allies had been defeated, and were glad to place a river between themselves and the Prussians. The Bavarians were, consequently, alone on the left bank of the Maine; their losses had been considerable; their *morale* was shattered; their retreat across the defiles of the Maine was insecure; and a defeat in their present position meant absolute ruin. The Prussian Official History says:

> A renewed attack on the part of the Prussian main forces would necessarily have forced it (the Bavarian Corps) to a struggle for life or death. The political situation of affairs showed no reason for bringing on so desperate a combat. The only object henceforth was to occupy as much territory of the allies as possible, in order to facilitate peace negotiations with them, and manoeuvring against the enemy's left flank would oblige him to retreat without any hard struggle.

This apology for a failure to complete the defeat of a shattered and unsupported hostile force seems somewhat disingenuous. A complete defeat and surrender of the Bavarians would have been quickly followed by the capture or dispersion of the VIIIth Corps, and the entire South-German territory would have been at the mercy of the Prussians. Certainly such a condition of affairs would have "facilitated peace negotiations" by rendering further resistance hopeless. Moreover, the same history states that the retreat of the VIIIth Corps behind the Maine was not known at the Prussian headquarters; and it seems probable that inefficient performance of outpost and reconnaissance duties on the part of the Prussians, rather than any considerations of politics or magnanimity, saved the Bavarians from destruction. Late in the day, Prince Charles withdrew across the Maine.

On July 27th the Prussians moved on Würzburg. Their artillery exchanged shots with the citadel of Marienberg (on the left bank of the Maine, opposite Würzburg), and succeeded in setting fire to the arsenal, but withdrew without effecting anything of moment.

The contending armies now faced each other, each in an almost impregnable position. The situation was, however, altogether in favour of the Prussians. Their communications were secure, while the communications of the allies with Hesse, Baden and Würtemburg were intercepted, and those with Bavaria were endangered, by the position of the Army of the Maine. Moreover, the Prussian IId Reserve Corps had moved from Saxony *via* Leipsic, Plauen and Hof, and was now approaching Baireuth. In the language of the Prussian Official History:

The position of the Bavarian Army at Würzburg had now become untenable. It could only extricate itself from its present position either by assuming the offensive against the Prussian army—which was scarcely possible at this point—or by a retrograde movement up the Maine, so as to face the army to the north and re-establish its base on the Bavarian territory in its rear.

But the bitterness of extreme defeat was not pushed home to the allies; for on July 28th news of the peace preliminaries between Prussia and Austria, and of an armistice with Bavaria, was received. Though the truce with Bavaria was not to go into effect until August 2nd, hostilities were suspended, the only movement of importance being the occupation of Nuremberg by the Prussian IId Reserve Corps.

Peace was concluded on August 13th with Würtemberg, on the 17th with Baden, and on the 22nd with Bavaria.

It is hardly possible to contemplate the operations of the armies in Western Germany, in 1866, with any feeling of admiration. In the strategical operations of Von Falckenstein and Von Manteuffel are found the only redeeming features of the campaign. Von Falckenstein especially, in pushing in between the two armies of the allies, and defeating them in succession, displayed generalship of no mean order; but the want of harmony between the allied leaders removed every obstacle from the path of Prussian success. The Prussians seem to have been often completely in the dark as to the designs, and even in regard to the positions, of the allies. We find the Army of the Maine waiting, in a defensive position, nearly two days, in ignorance of its own victory at Wiesenthal.

We find the Prussians winning a victory at Aschaffenburg, when their own unskilful march invited a defeat, and their success was due solely to the greater blunders of their opponents. Before, and even during, the Battle of Helmstadt the Prussians seem to have been in complete ignorance of the position and movements of Prince Charles, and Von Beyer's escape from disaster when surprised by the Bavarians, was due solely to the fact that the surprise was accidental and mutual. Advanced-guard, outpost and reconnaissance duties seem to have been performed with the grossest inefficiency. In almost every action the Prussians seem to have been unaware of the extent of their victory, or to have shown an incapacity to organise a pursuit. Gneisenau and his famous order to "pursue to the last breath of horse and man" seem to have been forgotten in the Army of the Maine; and we find Prince

Charles, after the Battle of Rossbrünn, quietly slipping back, without molestation, to an almost impregnable position, when a simple frontal attack by the Prussians would have completed the discomfiture and insured the destruction of the Bavarian Army.

As to the allies, every adverse criticism that can be made on their opponents, applies to them in a still higher degree. Their leaders rarely rose to the level of respectable mediocrity. The junction of the allied corps, which was imperative from the first, was made only when they were practically herded together by the movements of the Prussians. As soon as they had been forced into the long-desired junction, they voluntarily undertook an ill-advised movement which separated them again, at the very moment of their contact with the enemy. Incapacity and jealousy were characteristics of both the allied commanders; and to these defects Prince Alexander added the greater fault of insubordination. It would be hard to find among the improvised "political generals" who appeared on the stage of war in the earlier part of the American conflict, a single one who possessed in a greater degree than Prince Charles or Prince Alexander a genius for blundering—an eminent capacity for invariably doing the wrong thing. It may be said of the two generals of the allied armies, that their operations afford a fine demonstration of the principles of war by the method of *reductio ad absurdum*.

Appendix 3

Only a brief mention of the operations in Italy is here necessary. On the night of the 23rd of June, 1866, the Italian Army crossed the Mincio, and encountered the Austrians at Custozza on the next day. The Italian Army, numbering about 120,000 men, was under the nominal command of King Victor Emmanuel, the real commander being General La Marmora. The Austrians, numbering about 72,000, were commanded by Archduke Albrecht. The battle resulted in the defeat of the Italians, who withdrew across the Mincio. The Austrian commander remained on the defensive.

Garibaldi, with about 6,000 volunteers, invaded the Tyrol, but was defeated in two small actions. Though he finally succeeded in gaining a foothold on Austrian soil, his operations were of no importance.

On the 20th of July the Austrian fleet, under Tegethoff, defeated the Italian fleet in the great naval battle of Lissa, in which the Italians lost three iron clads.

Immediately after the Battle of Königgrätz, Venetia was offered by Austria to the French emperor, and the Vth and IXth Corps were recalled to the Danube. The Italians, under the command of Cialdini, again advanced, and the Austrians (now numbering scarcely 30,000) fell back to the neighbourhood of Venice. On the 25th of July all military operations were stopped by the conclusion of an armistice.

The Italians had everywhere suffered defeat. Yet their alliance was of the utmost advantage to Prussia; for they neutralized three army corps, which would have been of priceless value to the Austrians in Bohemia.

The Battle of Königgratz

By Charles Lowe

Not since the "*Völkerschlacht*," or Armageddon of the nations at Leipzig, in 1813, when the allies overthrew the hosts of Napoleon, had Europe witnessed such a stupendous conflict as was fought near Königgratz, on the Upper Elbe, in Bohemia, on the 3rd July, 1866. This battle was called of Königgratz by the Prussians, of Sadowa by the Austrians; and, as a matter of topographical fact, the latter was the more correct title, just as the field of Waterloo is known as Mont Saint Jean to the French, and Belle Alliance to the Prussians—in both cases with more justice. At Leipzig about 430,000 men had mingled in fight, while at Königgratz, as we shall call it in complement to our ancient and honoured allies the Prussians, the total number of combatants was about 435,000, or close on half a million of men.

What had called these armed hosts into the field? Briefly put, it was the question which was to be the leading power among the German-speaking peoples—Austria or Prussia. For centuries the former had asserted this position of proud pre-eminence, but there came a time when this claim of the Hapsburgs was no longer allowed by the great and growing monarchy of the Hohenzollerns. Austria wanted to have everything in Germany done after her particular way of thinking, and Prussia began to find it quite incompatible with her honour and her self-respect to be thus lorded over by a State which in many respects she deemed to be her inferior in point of light and leading.

Thus it came to pass that these two rival powers began to lead a very cat-and-dog life at the council-board of the Germanic Confederation of States; and Bismarck, who was the rising statesman of his time, prophesied that this condition of things could go on no longer, and that the only remedy for this eternal quarrelling between the two was a policy of "blood and iron" on the part of Prussia.

133

Once, however, they seemed to have suddenly become the best of friends. This was when they joined their forces, in 1864, to snatch Schleswig-Holstein, or the Elbe Duchies, as they were called, from the rule of the Danes. Bismarck was the great champion of "Germany for the Germans," and he thought it scandalous and unreasonable that a foreign people like the Danes should continue to domineer over the Teutons in the Elbe Duchies. Prussia and Austria, therefore, at his far-seeing instigation, combined to oust the Danes from the Duchies, and this they finally did after storming the Danish redoubts at Düppel.

But the worst of it was that the conquerors could not agree as to their spoil. Prussia wanted to do one thing with the Duchies, and Austria another. It is a common enough thing for thieves to fall out over the distribution of their booty, and this was precisely what the rival German Powers did with regard to Schleswig-Holstein. Bismarck, the long-headed statesman that he was, clearly foresaw that they must and would do so, and this was the very thing he wanted. He wished to have a good pretext for going to war with Austria, in order that this Power might be altogether excluded from the German family of nations, and that Prussia, taking her place, might inaugurate a new and better era for the Teutonic peoples.

Austria had fallen into the trap which he had laid for her, and she had no choice but to fight. Each, of course, claimed to be the injured party, and the old game of the wolf and the lamb was played over again to the amusement of all Europe. Some of the other German States sided with Austria, and some with Prussia, but the former were soon defeated and disarmed and then Prussia was free to direct her whole strength against the Austrians.

It was known that the latter were collecting all their strength in Bohemia, and King William, who had General von Moltke, the greatest soldier of his time, for his chief of the staff, or principal counsellor in affairs of war, resolved to make a dash into this province before its Austrian defenders knew where they were, and smite them, as David did the Philistines, hip and thigh. Accordingly, he divided the forces of his kingdom into three main armies, each composed of several army corps. The command of the First, or centre, Army, numbering about 93,000, was entrusted to the king's nephew, Prince Frederick Charles, called by his soldiers the "Red Prince," from the scarlet uniform of the Zieten Hussars which he generally wore; the Second, or left-hand Army, totalling 100,000 men, was given to the king's high-souled and chivalrous son, the crown prince, Queen Victoria's son-in-law; while the Third, or right-hand host, called of the Elbe, fell to General Herwarth von Bittenfeld, who fought throughout the campaign with a courage worthy of "Hereward, the last of the English."

But these three huge armies did not invade Bohemia in one overwhelming mass. Moltke, the great "battle-thinker," the "Silent One in Seven Languages," as his friends fondly called him, knew a trick worth two of that. His maxim was, "march separately, strike combined"; and yet it behoved him to keep the Austrians in perfect ignorance of where he meant to strike. The crown prince, on the left, started with his army from Silesia; the Red Prince set out from Lusatia, while Herwarth's point of departure was Thuringia.

Did Moltke himself also take the field? No, not at once; for it meanwhile sufficed this great military chess-player, this mathematical planner of victory, to sit quietly among his maps and papers at the offices of the Grand General Staff in Berlin, with his hand on the telegraph wire, and direct the movements of the three armies of invasion. Take the following description that was penned by an English witness of the crossing of the frontier by the army of the Red Prince:—

It was here (at a toll-house gate) that Prince Frederick Charles took his stand to watch his troops march over the border. He had hardly arrived there before he gave the necessary orders, and in a few moments the *Uhlans*, or lancers, who formed the advance guard of the regiments, were over the frontier. Then followed the infantry. As the leading ranks. of each battalion arrived at the first point on the road from which they caught sight of the Austrian colours that showed the frontier, they raised a cheer, which was quickly caught up by those in the rear, and repeated again, and again till, when the men came up to the toll-house and saw their soldier-prince standing on the border line, it swelled into a rapturous roar of delight, which only ceased to be replaced by a martial song that was caught up by each battalion as it poured into Bohemia. The chief himself stood calm and collected; but he gazed proudly on the passing sections, and never did an army cross an enemy's frontier better equipped, better cared for, or with a higher courage than that which marched out of Saxony that day.

Over the picturesque hills of Saxony, over the Giant Mountains into the fertile plains of Bohemia, swiftly sped the three superbly-organised armies like huge and shining serpents; and ever nearer did they converge on the point which, with mathematical accuracy, had been selected as the place where they would have to coil and deliver their fatal sting of fire. Hard did the Austrians try to block the path of the triune hosts and crush them in detail; but the terribly destructive needle-gun, with the forceful lance of the lunging *Uhlan* and the circling sabre of the ponderous *cuirassier*, ever cleared the way, and a series of preliminary triumphs marked the progress of the three armies towards junction and final victory. By the 29th the Red Prince had reached Gitschin, the objective point of the invasion, while his cousin the crown prince lay at Königinhof, on the left, a long day's march distant. Meanwhile the Austrians had all retired under the shelter of the guns of Königgratz, a strongly fortressed town on the left bank of the Upper Elbe, there to take their final stand, with their backs, as 'twere, to the wall.

The Austrians were commanded by Feldzeugmeister Benedek, and their army had been reinforced by the troops of the King of Saxony, who had sided with the foes of Prussia in the impending conflict, and were sure to give a good account of themselves. An equally stubborn resistance was to be expected from the Hungarian subjects of the Emperor Francis Joseph, who were second to none in all his polyglot dominions in respect of that ancient valour and other chivalrous qualities which had caused this gallant people to be called the "English of the East." Finer horsemen than the Hungarians existed in no army in all the world; and in this campaign, as in every other in which they had ever been engaged, the Austrians were particularly strong in cavalry. But, on the other hand, the Prussians were known to be armed with the lately-invented breech-loading needle-gun, while the Austrians still clung to the older-fashioned muzzle-loader, and professed to make light of their opponents' new-fangled rifle. They were soon to be shown convincingly which was the better weapon.

It was not till June 30th that King William and his *paladins*, Moltke, Bismarck, and von Roon, left Berlin by rail for the seat of war. They had scorned to witness the preliminary heats, so to speak, and only wanted to be present at the grand final. On July 2nd, after reaching Gitschin, which was near the headquarters of the Red Prince, Bismarck wrote to his wife:

> Just arrived from Sichrow. The field of battle there is still covered with corpses, horses, and arms. Our victories (so far) are greater than we thought. It appears that we have over 15,000

Konniggratz

prisoners, while the loss on the Austrian side is still greater in dead and wounded, being no less than 20,000. Two of the Army Corps are utterly scattered, and some of the regiments are wiped out to the last man. I have, indeed, up till now seen more Austrian prisoners than Prussian soldiers.

On the night of the same day (2nd July) King William, now in his seventieth year, had retired to rest in a little room of the "Golden Lion", which overlooks the market-place of Gitschin—a quaint little old town nestling among the hills of Northern Bohemia, on the southern side of the Giant Mountains. Wearied out with the fatigues of the day, he had hardly closed his eyes in sleep when he was unceremoniously woke up. His Majesty opened his eyes, and found Moltke standing by his bedside, the bearer of most important news, which General Voigts-Rhetz had just brought in from the Red Prince, whose headquarters were some six miles further to the east, at the chateau of Kamenitz on the Königgratz road. Voigts-Rhetz had first of all carried his momentous news to Moltke, who lodged on the opposite side of the square, and who was the real ruler of Prussia's battles, now and after in the French war. The king did nothing without consulting Moltke, nor did His Majesty ever issue an order that was not based on the well-thought-out advice of his chief of the staff.

The message of the Red Prince was of the very highest importance, for it upset all the resolutions which had previously been taken at the Prussian headquarters. Early in the day the exact whereabouts of the Austrians was unknown. It was *supposed* that they were on the left, or eastern, side of the Elbe, furthest from the Prussians, with their right and left flanks resting on two strong fortresses—Josephstadt and Königgratz, respectively—a position which it would have been terribly difficult, if not impossible, for their adversaries to assail; so that, pending the discovery of their real whereabouts, it had been resolved to let the Prussian troops rest on the 3rd, as they had been wearied out by their incredible feats of marching and fighting. Presently, however, "from information received," this resolution was revoked and replaced by another which deprived the fagged-out Prussians of the prospect of their much-needed day's rest; and a bold and rapid rider—Lieutenant von Norman—was despatched across country to the crown prince at Königinhof to ensure his cooperation with the Red Prince in a particular manner on the morrow.

But von Norman had barely started on his long and perilous ride when, lo and behold! another officer. Major von Ungar, came spurring in to the quarters of the Red Prince with a great piece of news. Attended by only a few dragoons, this officer had gone out scouting in the direction of Königgratz, and discovered that the bulls of the Austrian Army was without doubt on the right, or Prussian, side of the Elbe, holding a strong position on the further bank of the Bistritz brook, which ran very nearly parallel with the Elbe at a distance from it of some four miles.

MAJOR VON UNGAR CAME SPURRING IN WITH A GREAT PIECE OF NEWS

The position was strong, but not half so much so as the dreaded one beyond the Elbe, and the hearts of the Prussians jumped for joy. It seemed to them as if God had already delivered the Austrians into their hands, as Cromwell avowed of the Scots when they left their high ground at Dunbar and descended to meet his Ironsides on the plain. After gleaning this priceless intelligence, Von Norman had to ride for his life. A squadron of Austrian cavalry made a dash to catch him, but he rode like an English foxhunter, and only left behind him,

139

as a souvenir of his audacious visit to the enemy's lines, a part of his tunic which had been carried away by an Austrian lance-thrust.

This, then, was the news which Voigts-Rhetz had brought to Moltke and the king at Gitschin, and then the situation underwent an immediate and final change. It was resolved to assail the Austrian position early on the morrow with the whole force of the united Prussian armies, and another message to this effect, cancelling all previous ones, as a codicil does a will, was at midnight despatched to the crown prince on one hand and Herwarth on the other, informing them of the altered state of things, and desiring them on the morrow to assail the flanks of the Austrians as fast and furiously as ever they could; while the Red Prince would apply his batteringrams to their elevated and strongly entrenched centre. This urgent message was entrusted to Colonel von Finckenstein, who, after a very dark and dangerous ride of twenty miles, reached the crown prince's quarters about four o'clock on the morning of the 3rd July.

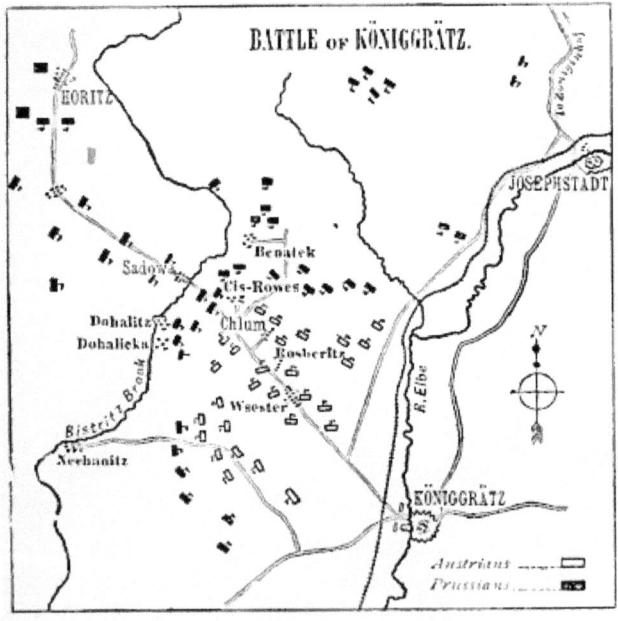

That fateful morning was a very wet and raw one, pretty similar to that which, after a rainy night, had dawned upon the English at Waterloo. Long before midnight the troops had all been in motion to the front. The moon occasionally blinked out, but was mostly hidden behind clouds, and then could be distinctly seen the decaying bivouac fires in the places which had been occupied by the troops along the road from Gitschin to Sadowa and Königgrätz. These fires looked like large will-o'-the-wisps as their flames flickered about in the wind and stretched for many a mile, for the bivouacs of so large a force as that of the Red Prince's army of nearly 100,000 men spread over a wide extent of country. With the first signs of dawn a drizzling rain came on, which lasted until late in the afternoon. The wind increased and blew coldly upon the soldiers, and they were short of both sleep and food, while frequent gusts bore down the water-laden corn on both sides of the ground along the way.

Moltke and his staff had left Gitschin by four o'clock, driving to Horitz, where, mounting their horses, they rode on to Dub and joined Prince Frederick Charles. For this was the centre point of assembly. The *Times* correspondent wrote:

> A few short words passed from the commander of the First Army to his chief of the staff; a few *aides-de-camp*, mounting silently, rode away; and, as it were, by the utterance of a magician's spell, one hundred thousand armed Prussian warriors, springing into sight as if from the bowels of the earth, swept over the southern edge of the Milowitz ravine towards the hill of Dub.

About eight o'clock, King William, with Bismarck and others of his great men, arrived upon the scene. Behind the king, besides his staff, were his royal guests, with their numerous retinues of adjutants and equerries, grooms and horses, in number equal unto about a couple of squadrons—making a fine mark for the shells of the Austrians. Before mounting his good mare "Fenella"—thenceforth to be called "Sadowa"—the king had got into his great-coat and put on galoshes over his boots. A wrong pair of spurs had been brought from Gitschin and would not fit. A groom whipped his off, and strapped them on over the royal galoshes; and thus equipped, with a field-glass slung round his neck by a long strap, the king rode away to view the course of the terrific fight, being everywhere received with tremendous cheering by his enthusiastic troops. For it touched their hearts to see so hoary a king come forth at the head of his "*Volk in Waffen*," or people in arms, to do strenuous battle with the alien. No *roi fainéant*, or stay-at-home monarch he, but one of the good old sort, like our own royal Edwards and Harries, under whose personal leadership the French were "beaten, bobbed, and thumped" at Crécy and at Agincourt.

It had been thought incredible by the Prussian leaders that the

Austrians should have waived the advantages of a position behind the Elbe, and come forward several miles on its hither bank so as to meet their adversaries on the terms of the latter. But a closer inspection of their line of battle showed that it had been singularly well chosen. Along their front ran the boggy Bistritz brook, its banks dotted with farmsteads, villages, and clumps of wood, forming fine cover for infantry; while beyond this the ground rose in gentle undulations till it finally assumed the appearance of a commanding swell or ridge, from which Benedek's batteries could pour down death and destruction on the advancing Prussians over the heads of his own infantry when engaging the helmeted wielders of the needle-gun.

GENERAL BENEDEK

From the top of the slight elevation whereon stands the village of Dub the ground slopes gently down to the Bistritz, which the road crosses at the village of Sadowa, a mile and a quarter from Dub. From Sadowa the ground again rises beyond the Bistritz to the little village of Chlum (mark that village!), conspicuous by its church-tower crowning the gentle hill, a mile and a half beyond Sadowa—a beautiful bit of country not unlike some parts of England with its hill and dale, clustering cottages, peeping *châteaux*, hedgerows, groves, and waving grain-fields. Profiting to the full by the defensive advantages of this terraced terrain, the Austrians had seamed it with entrenched batteries, and palisaded their approaches with felled trees and inter-twisted branches, making of the whole a natural fortress formidable to their assailants.

But nothing could daunt the hearts of the Prussians. They had got to beat Benedek and his 220,000 men, and the sooner the better. The Red Prince was afraid that, after all, Benedek might seek to retire behind the Elbe, and this had to be prevented at all costs and hazards. The prince might not be able to beat him off-hand, but he could at least fasten on Benedek like a bulldog and hold him fast there till the arrival of the crown prince, when the bull could be altogether felled and laid upon its back. *Bang*, therefore, went the Prussian batteries, and presently the whole sinuous line of battle, extending about five miles from Cistowes (opposite Chlum) on the Prussian left, to Nechanitz on the right, began to be wrapped in wreathed cannon smoke. The Austrians returned shot for shot, and neither side either gained or lost ground. In the centre the Prussians pushed battery after battery into action, and kept up a tremendous fire on the Austrian guns; but these returned it with interest, knowing the ground well, and every shell fell true, heaping the ground with dead and wounded men and horses.

While this furious cannonade was going on, columns of Prussian infantry were moved down towards the Bistritz, with intent to storm the line of villages—Sadowa, Dohalitz, and Dohalicka—on the fur-ther side. Shortly before their preparations were complete, the village of Benatek, on the Austrian right, caught fire, and the 7th Prussian Division made a dash to secure it; yet the Austrians were not driven out by the flames, and here, for the first time in the battle, it came to desperate hand-to-hand fighting.

But the bloody *mêlée* here was nothing to what was now mixing up the combatants in the wood of Sadowa, and converting it into a perfect slaughterhouse and hell upon earth. Boldly the Prussians ad-vanced upon this village and its wood, plying the rapid needle-gun with awful effect upon the wood's defenders. But nothing could have exceeded the splendid courage with which the Austrian battalions clung to their cover, and their volleys, supplemented as they were by a truly infernal fire from the batteries behind and above, seemed to mow down whole ranks of their assailants.

But neither bullets nor shells could decide the fierce struggle; the bayonet had to be called in to do this. And now ensued most horrible

The Prussians Pushed Battery after Battery into Action

scenes of carnage, which ended, however, before eleven o'clock, in the capture by the Prussians of the aforesaid villages. And no wonder that the Austrians chose to call the tremendous battle after the village and wood where they had made so glorious but ineffectual a stand.

Moltke himself afterwards related that, while he was watching the progress of events in front of Sadowa wood some roe-deer, startled from their leafy glades by the infernal pother around them, came bounding out and past him: and also how, when he and his suite rode forward a little way along the Lissa road to reconnoitre the Austrian position, he encountered an ownerless ox plodding along, serenely indifferent to the shells that were bursting all around it. Opposite the Sadowa wood on the Lissa heights, the Austrians had planted a most formidable entrenched line of guns, and Moltke afterwards told how he succeeded in getting the king to counter-order a command to storm these entrenched batteries from the front, which could only have ended in the bloodiest of disasters to their assailants.

About this time Bismarck, seeing how little headway the Prussians were making, began to be rather apprehensive as to the general result, fearing even that, if the crown prince came not up soon, they might, after all, be beaten. But one little incident gave him fresh hope. Taking out his cigar-case he offered a weed to Moltke, who deliberately chose the best of the lot. "Oh," thought Bismarck to himself, "if Moltke is calm enough to do that, we need have no fear after all."

The coming of the crown prince, with his additional hundred thousand men, had been as anxiously looked for as the arrival of Blücher on the field of Waterloo, and in truth the two situations were closely alike. Suddenly Bismarck, who had been looking intently in the crown prince's direction, lowered his glass and pointed to certain lines in the far distance, but these the others pronounced to be furrows.

"No," said Bismarck, looking again, "the spaces are not equal: they are advancing lines." And so they were; and by eleven o'clock the smoke of some Austrian batteries furnished a convincing proof that their fire was directed, not against the Red Prince's, but "Unser Fritz's" army; and the words "The crown prince is coming!" passed from lip to lip. But, sometime before his advance had thus been signalised, Moltke made answer to the king, who had been questioning him as to the prospects of the fight:

Today your Majesty will win, not only the battle, but also the campaign.

BOLDLY THE PRUSSIANS ADVANCED UPON THIS VILLAGE AND ITS WOOD

A correspondent with the Austrians wrote:

> The Prussian reserves were once more called upon; and from half-past twelve till nearly one o'clock there was an artillery fire from centre to left for six miles or more, which could not well have been exceeded by any action of which history makes mention. The battle was assuming a more awful and tremendous aspect, and the faint rays of sunshine which shot at intervals through the lifting clouds only gave the scene a greater terror.

About this time, also:

> Benedek and his staff passed through the 6th Corps, which was in reserve. As the green plumes were seen rapidly advancing, the bands broke forth into the National Anthem, and the men cheered their commander with no uncertain note. Faces broke into broad smiles; *Jäger* hats were thrown into the air; all seemed joyous in the anticipation of an approaching triumph. Benedek, however, waved to them to cease shouting, saying, in his peculiar tone of voice, 'Not now, my children: wait till tomorrow.'

And it was wise advice; for by this time Benedek had begun to suspect that he and his men would soon all have a very different song to sing.

The storm and stress of battle were now beginning to tell heavily on the Austrians. They were, it is true, still holding their own, or something like it, on the line of the Bistritz; but what is that which suddenly attracts the attention of Benedek and his staff behind the village of Chlum? They gallop away thither to inquire into the cause of all this new turmoil, and are greeted with a destructive volley from the needle-guns of "Unser Fritz," who had by this time, after a forced march of frightful difficulty across the sodden country from Königinhof, come upon the scene with his Guards, and not only turned the flank, but positively fastened on the rear of the Austrian fighting line, at which he was now hammering away with might and main. But his path, so far, had been encumbered with corpses and mutilated bodies in sickening masses, he wrote in his *Diary*:

> Around us lay or hobbled about so many of. the well-known figures of the Potsdam and Berlin garrisons. A shocking appearance was presented by those who were using their rifles as crutches, or were being led up the heights by some other

unwounded comrades. The most horrid spectacle, however, was that of an Austrian battery, of which all the men and horses had been shot down. . . . It is a shocking thing to ride over a battle-field, and it is impossible to describe the hideous mutilations which present themselves. War is really something frightful, and those who create it with a stroke of the pen, sitting at a green-baize table, little dream of what horrors they are conjuring up. . . . In Rosberitz, where the fight must have been frightfully bitter, to judge from the masses of dead and wounded, I found my kinsman. Prince Antony of Hohenzollern, who had been shot in the leg by three balls. (He died of his wounds soon after).

With the turning of the Austrian right by the crown prince, the battle was virtually won. On the extreme left, Herwarth had played similar havoc with the Saxons, in spite of the heroic desperation with which they fought; and by four o'clock the Prussian line of attack resembled a huge semi-circle hemming in the masses of battered and broken Austrian troops. Half an hour later the latter, perceiving that victory had at last been snatched from their grasp, began to give way all along their line; and then, with drums beating and colours flying, the Red Prince's men. with one accord, rose from their positions and began a general advance. Perceiving his opportunity, the king now gallantly placed himself at the head of the whole cavalry reserve of the First Army, which "charged and completely overthrew," to quote His Majesty's own words, a similar mass of Austrian horsemen.

The nature of the ground had hitherto prevented the cavalry of either army from acting in masses, but the country was more open on the line of retreat to Königgratz, and it now became the scene of several splendid lance and sabre conflicts. As the squadrons of the 3rd Prussian Dragoons were rushing forward to charge some Austrian battalions near the village of Wrester, an Austrian *Cuirassier* brigade, led by an Englishman of the name of Beales, charged them in flank. They drove the Prussians back, and, smiting them heavily with their ponderous swords, nearly destroyed the dragoons; but Hohenlohe's Prussian *Uhlans*, seeing their comrades worsted, charged with their lances couched against the Austrian flanks, and compelled them to retire. Pressed by the lancers they fell back, fighting hard, but then the scarlet Zieten Hussars charged them in turn in the rear. A fierce combat ensued, and the gallant Beales himself was borne wounded to the ground.

But all would not avail. The Austrians were in full flight towards the fortress of Königgratz, pursued by cavalry, volleyed at by infantry, and exposed to ever-increasing showers of shell-fire. Yet from some positions of advantage they continued to retaliate in kind; and it was while standing watching the pursuit that King William and his suite became exposed to a terrific counter-fire of shells. Bismarck, who was still with him, ventured to chide His Majesty for thus exposing his precious person so unnecessarily.

"Does your Majesty, then, think they are swallows?" asked Bismarck, on the king affecting to make light of the *whizzing* of shells and bullets.

Bismarck wrote to his wife:

No one would have ventured to speak to the king as I did, when a whole mass of ten troopers and fifteen horses of a *Cuirassier* regiment lay wallowing in their blood close to us, and the shells whizzed in unpleasant proximity to the king, who remained just as quiet and composed as if he had been on the parade-ground at Berlin.

In spite of all remonstrances the king would not budge, so, edging up on his dark chestnut behind the king's mare, Bismarck gave her a good sly kick with the point of his boot, and made her bound forward with her royal rider out of the zone of fire.

On coming up with the troops of the crown prince, the king had been nearly swallowed up by them for sheer joy. At sight of the venerable monarch, who had been exposing his person throughout the bloody fray like the most dutiful of his soldiers, battalion after battalion—some the mere shadows of their former selves—burst into frenzied cheering and rushed forward, officers and men, to kiss the hand, the boot, the stirrup of their beloved leader. But presently a scene more touching still was presented to the victorious Prussian troops, when the heroic crown prince rode up and met his father.

The crown prince wrote:

I reported to the king the presence of my army on the battle-field, and kissed his hand, on which he embraced me. Neither of us could speak for a time. He was the first to find words, and then he said he was pleased that I had been successful, and had proved my capacity for command, handing me at the same time the order '*Pour le mérite*' (highest of Prussian war decorations) for my previous victories.

GRAVESTONES ERECTED ON THE BATTLEFIELD IN MEMORY OF THE FALLEN.

Earlier in the day "Unser Fritz" had met his cousin the Red Prince.

> We waved our caps to one another from afar, and then fell
> into one another's arms amid the cheering of the troops of my
> extreme right and his extreme left wing . . . . Two years ago I
> embraced him as victor at Düppel; today we were both victors:
> for, after the stubborn stand made by his troops, I had come to
> decide the day with my army.

The battle had been won, but at what a terrible cost! Even the victors shuddered at the sight of the multitudes of bodies which heaped the bloody field. By superior arms, superior numbers, and superior strategy, Prussia, at the cost of 10,000 of her bravest sons, had won a crowning victory over her Austrian rival, who lost 40,000 men (including 18,000 prisoners), 11 standards, and 174 guns.

"I have lost all," exclaimed the defeated Benedek, "except, alas! my life!"

The highest proportion of the Prussian loss of 10,000 had fallen on Franzecky's Division, whereof 2,000, out of 15,000, had bitten the Bohemian dust. But *"Franzecky vor!"* ("Franzecky to the front!") will always live in the Prussian soldier's song as a memory of the everready leader who bore the brunt of the awful struggle on the line of the Bistritz.

That same night the king slept at Horitz—not upon a bed, but on his carriage cushions spread out on a sofa. Bismarck's couch was at first formed by a wisp of straw under the open colonnade of the same townlet, though afterwards he was invited to share the wretched room of the Grand Duke of Mecklenburg. Moltke rode back to Gitschin, a distance of about twenty miles from the battlefield, where a cup of weak tea was all the refreshment that could be got for him; and then, in a fever of fatigue, he threw himself down to sleep in his clothes, as he had to be up betimes and return to Horitz to procure the king's sanction for his further plans.

It was he, the "Great Silent One," who had won the greatest and most momentous battle of modern times.

It had taken Frederick the Great seven long years to humble the pride of Austria; it took William the Victorious, with Moltke as his "battle-thinker," but seven short days to achieve the same result. The Prussian soldier preferred to call the battle which he had just helped to win, Königgratz, because this name sounded to his ears as but a pun on the words *"Dem könig geräths"* ("The king will win"). But the

THE CROWN PRINCE RODE UP AND MET HIS FATHER

king had only won by acting on the sage advice of his all-calculating Moltke, whose motto was *"Erst wägen, dann wagen"*—that is, *"First weigh, then away!"*

LEONAUR

ALSO FROM LEONAUR

AVAILABLE IN SOFTCOVER OR HARDCOVER WITH DUST JACKET

ZULU:1879 *by D.C.F. Moodie & the Leonaur Editors*—The Anglo-Zulu War of 1879 from contemporary sources: First Hand Accounts, Interviews, Dispatches, Official Documents & Newspaper Reports.

THE RED DRAGOON *by W.J. Adams*—With the 7th Dragoon Guards in the Cape of Good Hope against the Boers & the Kaffir tribes during the 'war of the axe' 1843-48'.

THE RECOLLECTIONS OF SKINNER OF SKINNER'S HORSE *by James Skinner*—James Skinner and his 'Yellow Boys' Irregular cavalry in the wars of India between the British, Mahratta, Rajput, Mogul, Sikh & Pindarree Forces.

A CAVALRY OFFICER DURING THE SEPOY REVOLT *by A. R. D. Mackenzie*—Experiences with the 3rd Bengal Light Cavalry, the Guides and Sikh Irregular Cavalry from the outbreak to Delhi and Lucknow.

A NORFOLK SOLDIER IN THE FIRST SIKH WAR *by J W Baldwin*—Experiences of a private of H.M. 9th Regiment of Foot in the battles for the Punjab, India 1845-6.

TOMMY ATKINS' WAR STORIES: 14 FIRST HAND ACCOUNTS—Fourteen first hand accounts from the ranks of the British Army during Queen Victoria's Empire.

THE WATERLOO LETTERS *by H. T. Siborne*—Accounts of the Battle by British Officers for its Foremost Historian.

NEY: GENERAL OF CAVALRY VOLUME 1—1769-1799 *by Antoine Bulos*—The Early Career of a Marshal of the First Empire.

NEY: MARSHAL OF FRANCE VOLUME 2—1799-1805 *by Antoine Bulos*—The Early Career of a Marshal of the First Empire.

AIDE-DE-CAMP TO NAPOLEON *by Philippe-Paul de Ségur*—For anyone interested in the Napoleonic Wars this book, written by one who was intimate with the strategies and machinations of the Emperor, will be essential reading.

TWILIGHT OF EMPIRE *by Sir Thomas Ussher & Sir George Cockburn*—Two accounts of Napoleon's Journeys in Exile to Elba and St. Helena: Narrative of Events by Sir Thomas Ussher & Napoleon's Last Voyage: Extract of a diary by Sir George Cockburn.

PRIVATE WHEELER *by William Wheeler*—The letters of a soldier of the 51st Light Infantry during the Peninsular War & at Waterloo.